D0192738

The

FAITH

of Barack Obama

—— REVISED AND UPDATED ——

HILLSBORO PUBLIC LIBRARIES
Hillsboro, OR
Member of Washington County
COOPERATIVE LIBRARY SERVICES

ALSO BY STEPHEN MANSFIELD

Never Give In:
The Extraordinary Character of Winston Churchill

Then Darkness Fled:
The Liberating Wisdom of Booker T. Washington

Forgotten Founding Father:
The Heroic Legacy of George Whitefield

The Faith of George W. Bush

The Faith of the American Soldier

Benedict XVI: His Life and Mission

The Search for God and Guinness

Hillsboro, OR
Member of Washington County
COOPERATIVE LIBRARY SERVICES

The
FAITH
of Barack Obama
REVISED AND UPDATED

STEPHEN MANSFIELD

THOMAS NELSON
Since 1798

NASHVILLE   DALLAS   MEXICO CITY   RIO DE JANEIRO

HILLSBORO PUBLIC LIBRARIES
Hillsboro, OR
Member of Washington County
COOPERATIVE LIBRARY SERVICES

© 2008, 2011 by Stephen Mansfield

All rights reserved. No portion of this book may be reproduced, stored in a retrieval system, or transmitted in any form or by any means—electronic, mechanical, photocopy, recording, scanning, or other—except for brief quotations in critical reviews or articles, without the prior written permission of the publisher.

Published in Nashville, Tennessee, by Thomas Nelson. Thomas Nelson is a registered trademark of Thomas Nelson, Inc.

Thomas Nelson, Inc., titles may be purchased in bulk for educational, business, fundraising, or sales promotional use. For information, please e-mail SpecialMarkets@ ThomasNelson.com.

Scripture quotations marked NIV are from the HOLY BIBLE: NEW INTERNATIONAL VERSION®. © 1973, 1978, 1984 by International Bible Society. Used by permission of Zondervan Publishing House. All rights reserved.

Scripture quotations marked KJV are from KING JAMES VERSION.

Interior photos provided by AP Images.

Page design: Walter Petrie *4823 5468 3/12*

ISBN: 978-1-59555-463-5 (trade paper)

The Library of Congress has cataloged the hardcover edition as follows:

Mansfield, Stephen, 1958-
    The faith of Barack Obama / written by Stephen Mansfield.
        p. cm.
    Includes bibliographical references.
    ISBN 978-1-59555-250-1 (hardcover)
    1. Obama, Barack—Religion. 2. Presidential candidates—United States—Biography. 3. Legislators—United States—Biography. 4. Religion and politics—United States—Case studies. I. Title.
    E901.1.O23M36 2008
    328.73092—dc22
    [B]   2008023371

Printed in the United States of America

11 12 13 14 15 QGF 6 5 4 3 2 1

To Beverly, song of my life

Contents

The Life of Barack Obama: A Chronology

1961   Born in Honolulu on August 4 to eighteen-year-old Ann Dunham and Barack Obama Sr., the first African student at the University of Hawaii

1964   Barack's parents divorced when he was two years old

1966   Ann married Lolo Soetoro

1967   Barack and his mother moved to Indonesia

1971   Returned to Honolulu and enrolled in Punahou School

Ann and Lolo Soetoro divorced

1979   Entered Occidental University in Los Angeles

1981   Transferred to Columbia University in New York

1982   Barack Obama Sr. died in a car crash in Kenya at age fifty-two

1983   Graduated from Columbia University and went to work for Business International Corporation as a writer and analyst

1985   Began work with Developing Communities Project in Chicago

Began attending Trinity United Church of Christ

THE FAITH OF BARACK OBAMA

1987 Lolo Soetoro, Barack's stepfather, died of a liver ailment in Indonesia

Entered Harvard Law School at age twenty-seven

1990 Became the first African American president of the Harvard Law Review

1991 Graduated from Harvard and returned to Chicago

1992 Married Michelle Robinson

Stanley Dunham, Barack's grandfather, died

1993 Began work with Miner, Barnhill & Galland law firm in Chicago

1995 *Dreams from My Father* was released, to light praise and attention

On November 7, Ann Dunham Soetoro died of ovarian cancer

1996 Elected to the Illinois State Senate from Hyde Park

2000 Lost a congressional primary race against incumbent Bobby Rush

2004 On July 27, made the Democratic Convention speech that launched him to national prominence

On November 2, won the Illinois general election for U.S. Senate

Dreams from My Father was rereleased to wide acclaim

2006 *The Audacity of Hope* was released and became a best seller

2007 On February 10, announced his candidacy for president of the United States

2008 On November 4, was elected president of the United States

2009 On January 20, was inaugurated the 44th U.S. president

Introduction

It was August 18, 2010, and the lead story of the news cycle that day was not what the Obama White House wanted to hear. A new national survey conducted by the Pew Research Center revealed that a huge number of Americans were, at best, confused about President Obama's religious life and were, at worst, convinced he was lying about what he believed. Fully 43 percent of Americans said they had no idea what Obama's religion was. One third of all adults, some 34 percent, were convinced that Obama was indeed a Christian, as he claimed, but this was down sharply from 48 percent just a year before. And most disturbing of all, 18 percent said they were convinced that the president was a Muslim, which was not only up from 11 percent in March 2009, but represented nearly one-fifth of all Americans.[1]

Obama's senior advisors were stunned. How could this be? Surely Barack Obama had exposed his private faith to the public glare as much as any president in recent history. There had been not one but two best-selling books, *Dreams From My Father* and *The Audacity of Hope*, in which Obama had described his spiritual journey in heart-wrenching detail. Then there was the Reverend Jeremiah Wright controversy during the 2008 campaign that had led in turn to the "A More Perfect Union" speech, a high-water mark both for Obama's standing in the polls and for religious transparency by an American presidential candidate. There had also been the Presidential Faith Forum in which candidate Obama told Pastor Rick Warren of Southern California's Saddleback Church that he looked to Jesus Christ for the forgiveness of his sins. As if that wasn't enough, Obama had asked Warren to pray at his Inauguration, along with the ranking Bishop of the Episcopal Church.

Clearly, these public affirmations of faith, if the Pew Forum was to be believed, had made little impression on the public mind. What frustrated Team Obama even more, though, were the convincing displays of faith that went unreported, which a religiously unmoved media largely kept from public view. Why wasn't it widely known, for example, that each year since taking office Obama had given an Easter speech on his view of the resurrection of Jesus Christ that was so personal and passionate that it often left attendees in tears? Why didn't the press report that some of the most famous Christian leaders of the age helped encourage the president's faith. And to the charge that

Obama was still a Muslim, hadn't he said to the entire Islamic world—in his famous Cairo speech in June 2009—"I am a Christian." What more did this man need to do to declare his religion?

Still, the numbers did not lie. As one White House official said with exasperation, "Here we were slightly more than a year and a half into his presidency, just prior to the mid-term elections, and we find that nearly half of all Americans have no idea what Obama believes religiously. And a fifth think he's lying about being a Christian! We had failed and we knew it. We also knew the rules of the new game. A politician's faith is in play, part of the package, part of what gives him appeal. And because we knew this we knew we were in trouble."[2] And so they were. Less than three months later, Obama and his fellow Democrats received their famous "shellacking" in the mid-term elections, losing both prestige and control of Congress in one of the worst electoral defeats in American history. Polls revealed that religion had played a role—in the makeup of the influential Tea

> "Here we were slightly more than a year and a half into his presidency, just prior to the mid-term elections, and we find that nearly half of all Americans have no idea what Obama believes religiously. And a fifth think he's lying about being a Christian!"

Party, in the reason voters chose from the conservative side of the political spectrum, and in the suspicion and distrust with which many Americans viewed the Obama administration.

Equally troubling, Obama's senior staff and team of spiritual advisors knew they were dealing with something even more difficult to address than the Democratic Party's flagging political fortunes. They were dealing with a feeling, an amorphous sentiment, that Barack Obama was somehow other, that he was foreign, that he was far removed from the American religious mainstream. Some of this, of course, was a product of Obama's exotic background and his race, but it was also due to a deep-seated sense on the part of some Americans that the president simply was not who he said he was. This was as unfair, perhaps, as it was frustrating, but it was an obstacle of perception Obama's advisors knew they had to surmount.

For the already suspicious, evidence of the president's religious infidelity seemed readily at hand. After entering the White House, Obama and his family had chosen not to attend a Washington DC–area church since the chaos that ensued when they did made worship impossible. Instead, they attended services whenever they could at Evergreen Chapel, the small, nondescript sanctuary at Camp David, the president's private retreat. But this meant there were no pictures of the president exiting a church each Sunday while shaking the hand of a robed clergyman and waving—Bible in hand—to the press. Many Americans assumed the president simply stayed home on their Sabbath Day. Then there were the Jewish Seders and the Hindu

Diwali services and the Muslim Ramadan dinners that the Obama White House held. Many of these had been hosted even by the evangelical George W. Bush, but somehow a deeper suspicion attached itself to Obama when he invited non-Christian religions into the "President's House." Nor were Obama's political opponents any help when they made the kind of statements Mike Huckabee had offered to an American Family Radio interviewer in March 2011: "I have said many times, publicly, that I do think he [Obama] has a different world view, and I think it's in part molded out of a very different experience. Most of us grew up going to Boy Scout meetings, and you know, our communities were filled with rotary clubs, not madrassas."[3] Of course, there was no evidence that Barack Obama had ever darkened the door of a madrassa—an often radical school for Muslim youth—but it didn't seem to matter. Obama was of dark skin, from a darker family background and may well have been from the dark side spiritually. Any slur could be made to stick.

As convincing to those who distrusted Obama religiously were the president's actions in office. He seemed to never have heard of an abortion he did not support. He refused to take a stand for the Defense of Marriage Act. He supported the Palestinian cause—urging a return to 1967,

> *Obama was of dark skin, from a darker family background and may well have been from the dark side spiritually. Any slur could be made to stick.*

pre–Six Day War borders for the impending Palestinian state— rather than championing Israeli territorial integrity as other presidents had done. In short, Obama never seemed to grow his policies organically from the soil of faith, as Reagan or Bush or even Carter had attempted to do.

Obama advisors could scoff at such accusations but what they knew with certainty was that things had changed. They had lost ground in this matter of the president's religion and it was hurting them. They could blame the press secretary and his staff but they knew that the public relations apparatus of a presidential administration rarely handles the first family's religion well. The president's people are often clumsy in talking about the subject and the press is often clumsy in reporting it. It is seldom a winning game.

Still, they would have to reclaim the religious high ground. Nearly every one of their Republican opponents were people for whom religious faith was a frontline issue and each would be eager to flush Obama out. No, the questions about what the president believed and why he believed it were not going away. Indeed, they were going to intensify and perhaps serve to frame perceptions that would in time define the Obama presidency, both in the race for a second term and, perhaps, on the pages of history.

FACED WITH THESE MOUNTING RELIGIOUS CHALLENGES, IT was pleasant for some senior White House staffers—particularly those who had been with the president for many years—to think back to the early days, when an exciting young Barack Obama had announced himself and his religious intentions to an adoring nation. It had first occurred on a cool, overcast Tuesday in July 2004. On the afternoon of that day, Barack Obama had been making the expected round of meetings before his speech that evening at the Democratic National Convention in Boston. He had come at the request of John Kerry, who upon meeting Obama knew that the young man might very well be the face of the Democratic Party's future. Kerry wanted Obama's story and thoughtful oratory to feature in the convention's symbolic pageant just then unfolding before the watching world.

That afternoon, Obama walked the Boston streets with his friend, Chicago businessman Martin Nesbitt. At each stop, eager crowds formed and pressed ever closer to the thin black state senator from Illinois.

"This is incredible!" Nesbitt gushed. "You're like a rock star!"

Turning to his friend, Obama replied, "If you think it's bad today, wait till tomorrow."

Nesbitt looked puzzled. "What do you mean?"

"My speech is pretty good," Obama explained. Clearly, he already had some sense of his destiny.[4]

That evening, after being introduced by Illinois senator Dick Durbin as "a man who can help heal the divisions of our nation," Barack Obama strode to the rostrum to give the speech he was certain would resonate throughout the nation. Seventeen minutes later, he had decisively taken his place on the American political stage.

It was, by all accounts, the best speech of the convention, the kind that some politicians pray to give just once in their lifetimes. Though Obama did not shrink from extolling the superior heroism of John Kerry and the righteousness of Democratic Party values, he managed a tone that was somehow wise and apart. There was a nod to the limitations of government to solve problems, a call for an end to the political strife tearing at the nation's soul. Scripture and the poetry of the American experience surfaced gracefully, and all was infused with Obama's own story and what the promise of a "skinny kid with a funny name who believes that America has a place for him, too," might mean to others.

It was a masterful performance, and for those who listened to the speech with an ear for the overtones of faith, there was a single sentence that signaled a defining theme in Barack Obama's life.

> *"We worship an awesome God in the Blue States." Though the words are but nine among more than two thousand, Obama intended them as a trumpet call of faith.*

It came toward the end, at a moment when Obama criticized the pundits who divide the nation into red states, or those that lean conservative and Republican, and blue states, or those that tend to vote Democratic. At the beginning of a sweeping passage designed to reveal the folly of such labels, Obama exulted, "We worship an awesome God in the Blue States."

The sentence was nearly buried in the rhetorical flourishes that followed. Though the words are but nine among more than two thousand, Obama intended them as a trumpet call of faith. No longer, he was saying, would the political fault lines in America fall between a Religious Right and a secular Left. Instead, a Religious Left was finding its voice: *We, too, have faith*, they proclaimed. *Those of us on the political Left who believe in a woman's right to choose an abortion and who defend the rights of our gay friends and who care for the poor and who trust that big government can be a tool of righteousness—we also love God. We, too, have spiritual passion, and we believe that our vision for America arises from a vital faith as well. No longer will we be painted as the nonbelievers. No longer will we yield the spiritual high ground. The Religious Right has nothing on us anymore.*

It was a conscious attempt to reclaim the religious voice of the American political Left. Those nine words were meant to echo the footsteps of nuns and clergymen who marched with Martin Luther King Jr., of the religiously faithful who protested the Vietnam War or helped build the labor movement or prayed with César Chávez. Barack Obama was raising the banner of what he hoped would be the faith-based politics of a new generation, and he intended to carry that banner to whatever heights of power his God and the American people allowed.

THE FAITH THAT FUELS THIS VISION IS FASHIONED FROM the hard-won truths of Obama's own spiritual journey. He was raised by grandparents who were religious skeptics and by a mother who took an anthropologist's approach to faith: religion is an important force in human history—understand it whether you make it your own or not. Nurtured as a child in the warm religious tolerance of the Hawaiian Islands and the multiculturalism of Indonesia in the late 1960s and early 1970s, he grew into a young man for whom race was more of a crisis than religion. As the son of a white American mother and a black African father who left the family when Barack was only two years old, he felt too white to be at home among his black friends, and too black to fit easily into the white world of his grandparents and mother. He was a man without a country.

> *He was raised by grandparents who were religious skeptics and by a mother who took an anthropologist's approach to faith: religion is an important force in human history—understand it whether you make it your own or not.*

Ever the emotional expatriate, he was haunted by displacement through his college years and through his troubling experience as a community organizer in Chicago. It was not until he rooted himself in the soil of Trinity United Church of Christ on Chicago's South Side that he began to find healing for his loneliness and answers for his incomplete worldview. He experienced for the first time both connection to God and affirmation as a son of Africa. He would also be exposed to a passionate Afrocentric theology and a Christian mandate for social action that permanently shaped his politics. Through Trinity, he found the mystical country for which his soul had longed.

Yet he also found that through this country flowed a bitter stream. As he quickly came to understand, Trinity Church's broad Christianity was permeated by a defining, if understandable, spirit of anger: toward white America, toward a history of black suffering, and toward a U.S. government that consistently lived beneath the promise of her founding vision. If Obama himself refused to drink from this bitter stream, he was mentored by those who did. The senior pastor at Trinity, Dr. Jeremiah A. Wright Jr., had for decades given poetic voice to the anger of his people, and when his sermons reached the broader American public during the 2008 presidential campaign, it created the worst crisis of Obama's candidacy.

Still, besieged by critics from both the political Right and Left, Obama initially refused to abandon his pastor. Neither did he abandon his role as a champion of the Religious Left, and in this his timing was perfect, for the religious winds were just then shifting in American politics.

AS THE 2008 PRESIDENTIAL CAMPAIGN SEASON UNFOLDED, the Religious Right—the coalition of faith-based social conservatives that had defined the debate over religion in American politics for nearly three decades—was in disarray, if not decline. Jerry Falwell and D. James Kennedy, revered fathers of the movement, had recently died. Other leaders had been sidelined through scandal and folly. Ted Haggard, president of the influential National Association of Evangelicals, had fallen into disgrace through drug abuse and sexual immorality. Pat Robertson, once the leading voice of the Religious Right, had earned nationwide scorn when he called for the assassination of Venezuela's Hugo Chávez and then intimated that Israel's prime minister, Ariel Sharon, lay in a coma due to God's anger over Israeli "land for peace" policies. Clearly, the lions of the movement were passing from the scene, but a passing of the baton to a new generation of national leaders was nowhere in sight.

No longer unified and able to speak with one voice, the leaders of the Religious Right each went their own way in endorsing Republican candidates. Pat Robertson, long an antiabortion stalwart, endorsed Rudy Giuliani, the only pro-choice candidate among the Republicans. Bob Jones III, leader of the deeply fundamentalist Bob Jones University, endorsed the only Mormon candidate in the race, Mitt Romney. Longtime Religious Right kingmaker James Dobson issued statements attacking first Fred Thompson and then John McCain, only to endorse Mike Huckabee less than a month before the ex-governor dropped out of the race, much too late to have done any good. Strangely, few among the Religious Right seemed initially interested in Huckabee, a former Baptist preacher who spoke openly of his faith and extolled the virtues of faith-based politics. Of the remaining highly visible pastors in the nation, Joel Osteen and T. D. Jakes strained to remain nonpolitical, while Rick Warren and Bill Hybels went to great lengths to show that they were sensitive to and in some cases sympathetic with the priorities of the Religious Left, particularly as expressed by Barack Obama.

This fraying of the Religious Right was worsened by a surprising defection: evangelical voters, a mainstay of Republican politics for decades, began abandoning their party. By February 2008, esteemed pollster and cultural analyst George Barna was reporting that "if the election were held today, most born again voters would select the Democratic Party nominee for president." Though in the 2004 election George W. Bush had enjoyed a lopsided 62 percent of the "born again" Christian vote as opposed to the 38 percent who voted for John Kerry, by 2008 a mere 29 percent of born again voters were committed to Republican candidates. Some 28 percent were unsure of who they would vote for, while more than 40 percent had already chosen to vote for a Democrat.[5] Scandals, loss of leadership, and the declining fortunes of the Bush administration were prying evangelical voters from their traditional moorings just when candidate Barack Obama was proclaiming a new brand of faith-based politics.

Adding to the dissolving influence of the Religious Right were the religious preferences of a rising new generation whom demographers reported would be voting in record numbers. Polls indicated that the majority of Americans ages seventeen to twenty-nine intended to vote for a Democrat in 2008 and that

Barack Obama was their leading choice.[6] Moreover, it was not just his politics but his unorthodox spirituality that won them.

> When Obama speaks of questioning certain tenets of his Christian faith or the importance of doubt in religion or his respect for non-Christian religions, the majority of the young instantly relate and welcome his nontraditional faith as a basis for his—and their—left-leaning politics.

Religiously, the majority of America's young are postmodern, which means they do faith like jazz: informal, eclectic, and often without theme. They have largely rejected organized religion in favor of a religious pastiche that works for them. They think nothing of hammering together a personal faith from widely differing religious traditions, and many acquire their theology the same way they catch colds: through casual contact with strangers. Thus, when Obama speaks of questioning certain tenets of his Christian faith or the importance of doubt in religion or his respect for non-Christian religions, the majority of the young instantly relate and welcome his nontraditional faith as a basis for his—and their—left-leaning politics.

These three historic shifts—the loss of the Religious Right's national leadership, the drift of born-again voters toward the Democratic Party, and the religiously liberal, pro-Obama lean of young voters—changed the role of religion in the 2008 election. For a Religious Left just reclaiming its political voice, the marketplace of religious ideas in American politics was more open than at any time in a generation. It was a reality not lost on Barack Obama.

YET THAT WAS THEN, IN THOSE HEADY DAYS OF THE 2008 campaign when Obama's exotic life journey and the soul-searching it inspired were first attracting millions of Americans. They were drawn to him, in part, because his saga as he recounted it in his books and speeches contained all the wrenching, ancient themes of human history and literature: the longing for place, the yearning for a father, the hope for a destiny. In an unfathered, untethered generation, Obama seemed the Everyman in a heroic tale of spiritual seeking. Americans, as a people born of a religious vision, found in Obama at least a fellow traveler and at most a man at the vanguard of a new era of American spirituality.

Yet years into his presidency, the national mood had shifted. There had been a severe and disorienting recession. America was fighting three wars in three separate countries and none of them seemed to promise either victory for the U.S. and its allies nor long-term good for the lands in which they were fought. Political battles were conducted like blood feuds to the finish, reminiscent of the gladiatorial games of old. And a weariness or perhaps a bit of confusion had seemed to settle into Obama himself. His speeches no longer set audiences aflame. His promised change seemed an unachievable dream. In their disillusionment, many Americans began to suspect that Obama had failed them and had done so because he was not what he had claimed, was not in fact the young, destined warrior who had inspired them those years ago. Nor, perhaps, was he the man of *avant-garde* faith whom they had hoped would lead them in a new brand of faith-based politics.

These were the clouds that had formed over the Obama presidency by the time the results of that disturbing Pew Forum survey were revealed. The clouds were dark and threatened ill. What they obscured, though, was the transformation taking place in Obama's own spiritual life. Having left his church home of two decades just as he entered office and having chosen the quiet chapel at Camp David as his spiritual retreat—and having come under the influence of a new band of religious leaders—the president's first years in the White House were proving a season of religious deepening and refashioning. He was no longer as he was when he entered office. He was no longer a man shaped alone by twenty years in Jeremiah Wright's Chicago pew. Instead, he had changed, had been mentored by men of a different spirit. He was becoming a leader powered by a religious vision sure to surprise his political opponents, perhaps even sure to surprise some who had stood with him in the faith-based political battles of earlier days.

It is these themes, then—Obama's journey of faith, the religious torment that politics has thrust upon him, the spiritual refashioning he has undergone while in office—that are the focus of these pages. There is no attempt here to press a political agenda or to rage against the realities of Mr. Obama's life. Sufficient is the rage of current American politics. This book is instead written in the belief that if a man's faith is sincere, it is the most important thing about him, and that it is impossible to understand who he is and how he will lead without first understanding the religious vision that informs his life. Equally important, there are often such riches of beauty and wisdom to be gained from a life informed by faith that the contemplation of it becomes its own reward. This is the spirit in which this book has been written.

Still, Barack Obama is a political being, and there can be no shrinking from the political implications of his faith. That it should be done kindly and generously is the insistence of this book. That it must be done at all is an insistence of the current state of religion in American political life.

1

To Walk Between Worlds

BOBBY RUSH IS AN IMPRESSIVE MAN. BORN IN THE DEEP South town of Albany, Georgia, in 1946, he later moved with his family to Chicago, Illinois, and rose to become a United States congressman. Along the way, he served in the U.S. Army, earned a bachelor's degree and two master's degrees, became an ordained Baptist minister, and won such respect in his district on the South Side of Chicago that he is now in his tenth term in office.

He also has the courage of his convictions. He was a cofounder of the Black Panther Party in Illinois and spent years operating a medical clinic and a breakfast program for children. He was a pioneer in drawing attention to the agonies of sickle cell anemia in the black community. Not surprising given his track record, on July 15, 2004, Congressman Rush became only the second sitting U.S. congressman to be arrested—not for corruption or payola scams but for protesting human rights violations at the Sudanese Embassy in Washington DC.

Truly, Bobby Rush is an impressive man. So, why, in 1999, did thirty-eight-year-old Barack Obama, who had served in the Illinois senate only three years, decide to challenge Bobby Rush for his congressional seat? It could not have been the numbers. Rush's name recognition was more than 90 percent, while Obama's was barely 11. It also could not have been any political differences. Everyone knew that the two men held nearly the same views. It was one of the reasons that Rush often expressed hurt over Obama's challenge.

Whatever moved Obama to run against Rush, it was not a pleasant experience for the younger man. From the outset, Rush's approval rating was more than 70 percent. Then, not long into the campaign, Rush's son, Huey Rich, was tragically shot on his way home from a grocery store. The young man hung between life and death for four days. Though it was distasteful at the time for anyone to mention a political benefit to the tragedy, the outpouring of sympathy did seem to galvanize support for Rush, particularly among undecided voters. Soon billboards arose in the district, proclaiming, "I'm sticking with Bobby."

It never got better for Obama. Even President Clinton entered the fray and supported Rush, breaking his own policy of not endorsing candidates in primaries. Rush won with twice the vote Obama received—approximately 60 percent to 30 percent—and Obama was forced to admit "[I got] my rear end handed to me."

There had been hurt and bitterness—the bad blood that fierce political battles can leave between men. Years went by, though, and with distance came a mellowing. The same Rush who had once described Obama as a man "blinded by ambition" came, in time, to a different view. After Obama entered the U.S. Senate, Rush said, "I think that Obama—his election to the Senate—was divinely ordered. I'm a preacher and pastor. I know that was God's plan. Obama has certain qualities. I think he is being used for some purpose."[1]

This confidence was not unique to Bobby Rush. Both during his years in the U.S. senate and then during his campaign for president in 2008, words such as *called*, *chosen*, and *anointed* were frequently used of Barack Obama. These terms had long been part of the native language of the Religious Right. They soon became, though, the natural expressions of an awakened Religious Left, of a faith-based Progressive movement. Moreover, they helped to frame the defining image of Barack Obama in the minds of millions of Americans.

> *"I think that Obama—his election to the Senate—was divinely ordered. I'm a preacher and pastor. I know that was God's plan. Obama has certain qualities. I think he is being used for some purpose."*

Yet what is unique about the use of such terms as applied to Barack Obama is how foreign they are to the religious worldview of his early life. We must remember that Obama is the first American president not raised in a Christian home. Instead, he spent his early years under the influence of atheism, folk Islam, and a humanist's understanding of the world that regarded religion merely as a man-made thing, as a product of human psychology. It is this departure from tradition in Obama's early years that makes both his political and religious journey of such widespread fascination and symbolic meaning in American public life.

THE STORY OF THE RELIGIOUS INFLUENCES THAT HAVE shaped Barack Obama is best begun with the novel faith of his grandmother, Madelyn Payne. She was born in 1922 to strict Methodist parents in the oil boom town of Augusta, Kansas. Though modern Methodists are known more for their eagerness to accommodate the sensitivities of secular society—removing offensive "gender bias" from their hymns, for example—the Midwest Methodists of the 1920s and 1930s exacted a higher price for righteousness. There was no drinking, card playing, or dancing in the Payne household. In church on Sundays, the family heard often of how small the army of the saved truly is compared to the vast numbers of those in the world who are going to hell. There were, too, the petty tyrannies that often attend religion in a flawed world: people shunned one another, lived lives at odds with the gospel they claimed to hold dear, and failed to distinguish themselves in any meaningful way from the world around them.

These hypocrisies were not lost on Madelyn Payne. She would tell her grandson often of the "sanctimonious preachers" she had known and of the respectable church ladies with absurd hats who whispered hurtful secrets and treated those they deemed beneath them with cruelty. What folly, she would recall with disgust, that a people would be taught to ignore all the geologic evidence and believe that the earth and the heavens had been created in seven days. What injustice, she would insist, that men who sat on church boards should utter "racial epithets" and cheat the men who worked for them. Barack regularly heard such bitter sentiments in his grandparents' home, sentiments that profoundly shaped his early religious worldview.

Madelyn was frequently described by neighbors as "different," a gentle word for her eccentricities, and few were likely surprised when she met, and then secretly married, Stanley Dunham, a furniture salesman from nearby El Dorado. If the marriage was not exactly the attraction of opposites, it was at least the blending of incongruities. He was notoriously loud, crashing, and gregarious; friends said he could "charm the legs off of a couch." She was bookish and sensitive. He was a Baptist from a blue-collar world. She was a Methodist whose parents were solidly middle class. Though in their generation these seemingly slight differences were enough to separate couples of less determination, Stanley and Madelyn fell in love and later married on the night of a junior/senior prom just weeks before her high school graduation in 1940. For reasons that remain unclear, her parents were not told of the union until her diploma was well in hand. They did not receive the news well, though this seemed to make little difference to the headstrong and increasingly rebellious Madelyn.

With the onset of World War II, Stanley enlisted in the army and ended up slogging through Europe with General George Patton's tank corps without ever seeing real combat. Madelyn worked as a riveter at the Boeing Company's B-29 plant in Wichita. In late November 1942, their daughter, Ann Dunham, was born.

Stanley Dunham has been described as a kind of Willy Loman, the tragic, broken character in Arthur Miller's *Death of a Salesman*. There are similarities. Returning from war and grasping the promise of the GI Bill, Stanley moved his young family to California, where he enrolled at the University of California Berkeley. Obama would later recount kindly of his grandfather that "the classroom couldn't contain his ambitions, his restlessness, and so the family moved on."[2] It was the pattern of a lifetime. There was first a return to Kansas and then years of one small Texas town after another, one dusty furniture store leading to the promise of bigger rewards at still another store farther up the road.

Finally, in 1955, just as Ann finished the seventh grade, the family moved to Seattle, where Stanley acquired a job as a salesman for Standard-Grunbaum Furniture, a recognized feature of the downtown area at the corner of Second and Pine. For most of their five years in Seattle, the family lived on Mercer Island, "a South America-shaped stretch of Douglas firs and cedars," which lay across from the city in Lake Washington.[3] While Stanley sold living room suites and Madelyn worked for a bank, young Ann began drinking from the troubled currents of the counterculture just then beginning to sweep through American society.

The high school that Ann attended was far from the stereotypical 1950s image. In the very year that she began classes at Mercer High, John Stenhouse, chairman of the school's board, admitted before the House Un-American Activities Subcommittee that he was a member of the Communist Party. Already at Mercer, there were recurring parental firestorms over the curriculum, long before such conflicts became commonplace throughout the nation. Most complaints centered on the ideas of Val Foubert and Jim Wichterman, two instructors who were perceived as so radical for the time that students called the passageway between their classrooms "Anarchy Hall." Together the two men had determined, without apology, to incite their students to both question and challenge all authority.

Foubert, who taught English, assigned books such as *Atlas Shrugged*, *The Organization Man*, *The Hidden Persuaders*, *1984*, and the most strident of H. L. Mencken's cultural commentaries—none of which are extreme by today's standard but which were certainly out of the mainstream in 1950s America.

Wichterman, who taught philosophy, assigned Sartre, Kierkegaard, and Karl Marx's *The Communist Manifesto*, and did not hesitate to question the existence of God. Parental upheavals ensued, which Foubert and Wichterman dubbed "Mother Marches." "The kids started questioning things that their folks thought shouldn't be questioned—religion, politics, parental authority," John Hunt, a student at the time, remembered, "and a lot of parents didn't like that and tried to get them [Wichterman and Foubert] fired."[4]

None of this upheaval was of much concern to Stanley and Madelyn Dunham, though. Having long before shed the quaint faith and suffocating values of rural Kansas, Ann's parents were comfortable with the innovations in the Mercer High School curriculum. They had even begun attending East Shore Unitarian Church in nearby Bellevue—often referred to in Seattle as "the little Red church on the hill"—for its liberal theology and politics. Barack would later describe this as the family's "only skirmish into organized religion" and explain that Stanley "liked the idea that Unitarians drew on the scriptures of all the great religions," excitedly proclaiming, "It's like you get five religions in one!" "For Christ's sake," Madelyn would shoot back, according to Barack, "It's not supposed to be like buying breakfast cereal!"[5]

Though what has come to be known as the Unitarian Affirmation of Faith is, in fact, an overly simplistic reworking of the ideas of James Freeman Clarke, it does serve to hint at what the Dunhams accepted as true: "the fatherhood of God, the brotherhood of man, the leadership of Jesus, salvation by character, and the progress of mankind onward and upward forever." That Stanley and Madelyn believed in a God of some description is confirmed by Barack. However, they were likely skeptics—Barack says that Madelyn espoused a "flinty rational-ism"—regarding the divinity of Jesus, whom they would have accepted as one good moral teacher among many but certainly not a god. That man is perfectible, that men ought to live as brothers, and that society would climb ever upward if they did are all truths that were agreed upon in the Dunham home, though Ann would in time accept these possibilities only on the most secular terms.

In truth, Ann Dunham was already on a journey beyond the freethinking of her parents, beyond her friends at Mercer High School, and yet in keeping with the philosophical trends of her times. She had absorbed the broad spirituality and social vision of the East Shore Unitarian Church. She had also been paying

> Though what has come to be known as the Unitarian Affirmation of Faith is, in fact, an overly simplistic reworking of the ideas of James Freeman Clarke, it does serve to hint at what the Dunhams accepted as true: "the fatherhood of God, the brotherhood of man, the leadership of Jesus, salvation by character, and the progress of mankind onward and upward forever."

attention in the classrooms of Foubert and Wichterman. Having begun with her parents' religious skepticism, Ann went even further and declared herself an atheist.

During after-school gab sessions in the coffee shops of Seattle, her friends began to realize how fully Ann had thought through her beliefs. "She touted herself as an atheist, and it was something she'd read about and could argue," remembers Maxine Box, who was Dunham's best friend in high school. "She was always challenging and arguing and comparing. She was already thinking about things that the rest of us hadn't." Another classmate, Jill Burton-Dascher, recalls that Ann "was intellectually way more mature than we were and a little bit ahead of her time, in an off-center way." "If you were concerned about something going wrong in the world," Chip Wall, a friend, explains, "[Ann] would know about it first." She was, he says, "a fellow traveler. . . . We were liberals before we knew what liberals were."[6]

As the decade of the 1960s dawned and Ann approached the end of her high school career, friends expected she might chart a bold course: college at a European university perhaps, or studies back east among the nation's Ivy League. They soon heard that Stanley had found a new job—yet another furniture store with yet brighter promises of success—this time in Hawaii. Though some remember that Ann did not want to go, it was not long before letters began arriving from Honolulu, describing how she had enrolled in the University of Hawaii for the fall term of 1960.

Only the year before, Hawaii had achieved statehood. This was likely part of the attraction for Stanley. His adventurous, ever-unsatisfied soul yearned for what appeared to be a new frontier. A fresh start in a new state, far from the American mainland, seemed ideal. He was entering his forties—the onset of midlife crisis for most men—his only daughter had just finished high school, and the darkness of the 1960s had yet to descend. Life was full of promise, though for Stanley this would mean going where that promise lived: a new place, a new role, a new crowd to charm.

He could not have known that it would be the last move of his life or that he would eventually pass his days in a small Honolulu apartment, if not embittered then at least disillusioned by his few achievements. He could not have known that in the meantime, his wife would rise to become the first female vice president of the Bank of Hawaii and would do so without a college degree, an astonishing achievement for a woman in that era. And he could not have known that his life would be both graced and anguished by the comings and goings of his daughter and the little biracial boy she would bring into the world.

⁓

Ann Dunham met Barack Obama Sr. while she was a freshman and he a graduate student at the University of Hawaii. He must have appeared exotic to her, with his rich, full voice; his Kenyan accent; his chiseled features; and his studied worldliness. He had come to Hawaii on the wings of extreme good fortune: his government had sent him abroad to study on a scholarship created for the rising leaders of Jomo Kenyatta's Kenya. Though he now spent weekends with Ann, listening to jazz, drinking beer, and debating politics and world affairs with their friends, he had only a few years before lived a Kenyan village life, herding goats and submitting to the rituals of a village witch doctor. Now, in the West, he had rejected the Muslim faith of his youth just as he rejected the babblings of all witch doctors. Religion is superstition, he insisted. It falls to man to fashion his own fate and the fate of his nation. This was what he intended to do when he finished school and returned to Kenya.

Things moved quickly for Ann and her new love. Sometime late in the fall of 1960, she conceived a child. Several months into 1961, she and Barack married, and six months later, friends in Seattle were receiving letters announcing the birth of their son, Barack Hussein Obama, born August 4, 1961.

What followed immediately after is now well known. Barack Obama Sr. continued to live in Hawaii only a short time after the birth of the son who bore his name. An opportunity to earn his doctorate at Harvard proved too enticing, and he left to return only once more before his death in 1982 of alcohol, bitterness, and a car crash. The pictures of young Barack make it hard to imagine any father walking away from such a child. In time, Ann and Barack would learn that Barack Sr. had been married in a Kenyan village ceremony long before he met Ann and already had other children. She would file for divorce in 1964.

There are many things to admire about Ann and how she raised her son, and certainly among them is the way she kept the positive memory of Barack Obama Sr. alive in her son's heart. Though a less generous soul might speak only ill of such a man, Ann regularly rehearsed his virtues to young Barack. The boy knew nearly from birth that his father had grown up poor in a poor country on a poor continent, and that only through hard work and toughness had he risen to esteem. "Your brains, your character, you got from him," she assured him, and so worked to keep a deforming bitterness from settling into her son's spirit.

> There are many things to admire about Ann and how she raised her son, and certainly among them is the way she kept the positive memory of Barack Obama Sr. alive in her son's heart.

The years after Barack Sr.'s departure, and while the family was still in Hawaii, were nearly idyllic for young Barack. There were frequent trips with Grandfather Stanley to the Ali'i Park, joyous days at the beach, and adventures such as deep-sea fishing off Kailua Bay that seared themselves happily into his memory. A photograph survives from this time of Barack swinging a baseball bat nearly as long as he is. It is an image of a child who is loved and content, a picture taken by a member of the family who clearly delights in those spindly legs, that broad smile, that beautifully shaped head. Madelyn, whom young Barack called "Toot"—short for the Hawaiian word for grandmother, *Tutu*—read to her grandson by the hour, eager to pass along the literary joys she had known as a child through the Great Books her family ordered by mail on the plains of Kansas. These were happy times. The haunting of race, rootlessness, and an absent father are for later years.

Creeping into Barack's remembrance of these years is a man named Lolo Soetoro, a friend and a fellow student of his mother's at the University of Hawaii. He soon after became Barack's wrestling partner and Stanley's loyal opponent in chess. Within two years, he was more, and Ann told her son that Lolo had proposed marriage, that she had accepted, and that it meant they would move to the other side of the world, to a place called Indonesia.

It says much about Ann Dunham Soetoro that she would uproot her son from the glories of Hawaii and move him in the mid-1960s to one of the most troubled places on earth. Indonesia had been led for decades by its revolutionary founder, Sukarno, a man more adept at words than administration. He had attempted to build his country on five ideals he called the Five Fundamental Principles: nationalism, internationalism, democracy, social prosperity, and belief in God. These were intended to be the essence of the Indonesian spirit. However, Sukarno's era in Indonesia is testament that words alone do not make a nation. By the 1960s, Sukarno's ineptitude had led to widespread suffering. As historian Paul Johnson has written: "Food rotted in the countryside. The towns starved. Foreign investment vanished."[7] Meanwhile, Sukarno's personal behavior became an international scandal. He acquired wives and mistresses freely, and his foreign jaunts were famous for his sexual foraging. During a visit to Indonesia in 1960, Soviet premier Nikita Khrushchev was shocked to see Sukarno chatting happily and openly with a completely naked woman.[8]

To cover the disasters of his leadership, Sukarno secretly gave the nod to a coup by the Communist Party in 1965. Sukarno's generals and handpicked officials were murdered, their daughters raped, the bodies of their wives and children thrown into the Lubang Buaja, the Crocodile Hole. The coup failed, however, and a General Suharto, the strategic reserve commander, took over. In a bloody backlash against the communists, hundreds of thousands were butchered, perhaps as many as a million. These horrors slowed to an end in 1966, only a year before Ann began to raise her six-year-old son in Jakarta.

The years that young Barack's family lived in Indonesia will likely remain among the most controversial of his life.

The years that young Barack's family lived in Indonesia will likely remain among the most controversial of his life. The facts are simple enough, though. The family initially resided in a small, flat-roofed bungalow at 16 Haji Ramli Street. Barack, who was known as Barry in these years, ran the dirt streets around his house, wearing a sarong, the traditional wraparound skirt worn by men, and played soccer by the hour with the neighborhood children. Because Lolo, his stepfather, was a Muslim, young Barry was listed as Muslim in official documents. Occasionally, he accompanied Lolo to a nearby mosque on Fridays and prayed at his side for the blessings of Allah.

In 1968, Barry began first grade at St. Francis Assisi Foundation School, which was a few blocks from his home. As each school day began, he would cross himself, pray the Hail Mary, the Our Father, and whatever else the attending nuns required. The atheist Ann and the Muslim Lolo endured this Catholic influence because the education at the school was among the best available. Two years later, after Lolo landed a job with an oil company and moved the family to a better neighborhood, Barack entered a public school now called Model Primary School Menteng 1. Here again, Barack was listed as a Muslim, which meant that he studied the doctrines of Islam during the required two hours a week of religious instruction.

His life was a religious swirl. He lived in a largely Muslim country. He prayed at the feet of a Catholic Jesus. He attended a mosque with his stepfather and learned Islam in his public school. At home, his mother taught him her atheistic optimism. She was, wrote Obama years later, "a lonely witness for secular humanism, a soldier for New Deal, Peace Corps, position-paper liberalism."[9]

Lolo's faith was more complex. Though he called himself a Muslim and urged Islam on Ann and Barack as a means to connect to the community, he was not very religious. This is surprising to many contemporary Westerners who think of Islam only in terms of the strident, fundamentalist strain that is causing so much heartache in the world today. Indonesia in the late 1960s and early 1970s was often violent for political reasons, but seldom for the sake of religion. The Islam of Indonesia in those days easily blended with Hinduism, Buddhism, and even animism, to produce a broad, eclectic spirituality. The daily experience of this blend is best described as folk Islam, a superstitious and occult fringe faith comprised largely of rituals to drive away evil: incantations against the evil eye, charms to ward off spirits, symbols to assure blessing, and ancient understanding of spiritual power and its uses.

Lolo lived on the folk edge of Islam, teaching young Barack superstitions and rituals popular on the streets of Jakarta. He believed, for example, that a man took on the powers of whatever he ate, a cherished pagan notion through the centuries. He often brought tiger meat home in hopes of making his stepson a fiercer, more powerful man. Yet the doctrines of orthodox Islam held little sway with Lolo. For example, he employed a young male cook who liked to dress up as a woman on weekends, something a more faithful Muslim would never have allowed in his home. Indeed, the young man's life would have been in peril among fundamentalists. Lolo also loved women, drink, and Western music. Barack would later recall his stepfather's passion for Johnny Walker Black and Andy Williams records. "Moon River" was nearly the soundtrack of his Indonesian memories.

Obama has written that his mother taught him to view

> Obama has written that his mother taught him to view religion as "a phenomenon to be treated with a suitable respect, but with a suitable detachment as well."

religion as "a phenomenon to be treated with a suitable respect, but with a suitable detachment as well."[10] It is just this detachment that may have proven the greatest emotional lesson of his years in Indonesia. He was to live in a Muslim country but be taught by his step-father's example to ignore the most fundamental teachings of Islam. He was to attend a Roman Catholic school, but regard Christianity as no more than superstition. And he was to love a mother who viewed all religion as nothing more than a man-made tool for contending with the mysteries of life. Only through a steely shielding of the heart, only through a determined detachment, could a child of Barack's age be exposed to so much incongruous religious influence and emerge undamaged. Perhaps, though, the damage was in the detachment itself.

THE QUESTION THAT WILL SURFACE AGAIN AND AGAIN about Obama's years in Indonesia is this: Was Barack Obama a Muslim? If he was a true Muslim, then his conversion to Christianity in his later years would make him *murtadd* in the eyes of Muslims: an apostate. Orthodox Islam would insist that such a man be rejected by his community and, in some jurisdictions, marked for death.

This extremism regarding apostates is not buried in an ancient age of Islam but is still very much alive today and has actually intensified in recent decades. The revered and controversial Pakistani scholar Sayyid Abul Ala Maududi, for example, argued fiercely in the mid-1990s for the execution of apostates, and his thinking is typical of the reasoning that might be applied to Barack Obama's story:

> The heart of the matter is that children born of Muslim lineage will be considered Muslims and according to Islamic law the door of apostasy will never be opened to them. If anyone of them renounces Islam, he will be as deserving of execution as the person who has renounced *kufr* [infidelity to Islam] to become a Muslim and again has chosen the way of *kufr*. All the jurists of Islam agree with this decision. On this topic absolutely no difference exists among the experts of *shari'ah*.[11]

The question of whether Obama fits this description is complicated somewhat by the way a man becomes a Muslim. In Islam, a man submits to Allah and enters the community of faith by reciting the creed, the *Shahadah*: "There is no God but Allah, and Muhammad is his Prophet." These are the words a Muslim speaks over his newborn child and hopes to have upon his own lips at his death. They are the keys to faith, the pathway of conversion.

Did young Barack say these words in honor of Islam? Yes, certainly, both at his stepfather's side in the Jakarta mosque on Fridays and in the Islamic religious instruction he received several hours a week in school. Does this make him a Muslim in his childhood and therefore a *murtadd* now? Neither the Koran nor the *Hadith*, the systematic compilation of Muslim teaching, addresses this issue with certainty. The question seems to vary from jurisdiction to jurisdiction, but the majority opinion among Islamic teachers, despite Maududi's insistence to the contrary, is that a child must have reached puberty before his confession of faith amounts to a full conversion. Young Barry was years from puberty in his last months in Indonesia—before he returned to America where he never practiced Islam again— so he is not to be considered a full convert to Islam, and therefore he is not an apostate now.

It is an interesting question, and one that will likely surface often. If, as president, Mr. Obama should offend some Islamic mullah by his policies, there could conceivably be a *fatwa* [religious decree] issued against him from a renegade jurisdiction on the basis that he is an apostate. It would be untrue, of course, in light of the consensus of Islamic teaching. Still, some enraged mullah might take note that Obama's biological father was an apostate from Islam. This could be held alongside Obama's own childhood confession of faith as sufficient evidence to rule him a *murtadd* and thus deserving of death. It would all be a lie, of course, and nothing more than a manufactured excuse for murder. Nevertheless, it would be the first time in American history that such a charge could be engineered against a sitting president.

Though religion permeated Barry's years in Indonesia, what may have had an even greater impact on the course of his life were his mother's efforts to give him a superior education. This came in the wake of a decline in Ann and Lolo's relationship and her realization that she did not want to lose Barack to Indonesia. She long had preached the virtues of cultural sensitivity, of never becoming a boorish outsider to the indigenous people. Now, she began to fear that the tentacles of this strange land were wrapped too tightly around her son. No, she would not lose him to the East. He would be an American, she determined, and education was the best way to make this so.

From the time they arrived in Jakarta, she had supplemented his local schooling with a correspondence course from the States. Now determined to seal her son to the West, Ann redoubled her efforts. Each morning, she awakened Barry at 4:00 a.m., fed and dressed him, and began drilling him in English for three hours before he traipsed off to school. It was not a pleasant experience. Barry resisted, claimed illness, and generally fought his mother at every step. In time, the lessons took hold, and Barry began to show a facility for language and learning that surprised even Ann. Though it could not have seemed the case at the time, these early morning sessions and the mental rigors they required may well have been the spark of the intellectual fires that gave him, ultimately, an exceptional mind.

These efforts are evidence that Ann had set her heart upon

returning to America. And so she did. Obama's little sister, Maya, was born, and not long afterward Ann made plans for Barack to return to the States. Ann and Maya initially remained in Indonesia and then in a matter of months returned, gratefully, to the United States. There followed a divorce. The three—Ann, Barack, and Maya—would see Lolo only once more in their lives, when he traveled to Los Angeles ten years later for treatment of the liver ailment that ultimately killed him at the age of fifty-one.

Upon his return to Honolulu in 1971, Barack was enrolled in the esteemed Punahou School. It was a turning point in his young life, one that determined much that would follow. Until then, other than the intelligence his mother recognized in him, there seemed to be little exceptional about his life. He lived with middle-class grandparents and followed his quixotic mother as she chased her loves and her dreams. He was a bright ten year old, but nothing as yet indicated the promise of his life: nothing concretely presaged the ascent to come. Punahou was the beginning of distinction.

He gained admission through the good graces of his grandfather's boss, an alumnus of the school. After interviews and testing, Barack was admitted and thus became part of a tradition that dated to 1841, when Punahou was founded to educate the children of Hawaii's Congregational missionaries. In the more than a century and a half since, it had become "an incubator for the island elites."[12] Barack was a student there for a vital seven years of his life. Academically and athletically, he thrived.

He maintained a solid B average, threw himself into his love of basketball, and even wrote for the school's literary magazine.

Yet in these years he also began the agonizing search for belonging as a man of mixed race. Who was he really? What tribe could he claim as his own? Mixed in with his natural adolescent search for both freedom and definition was a more subterranean yearning to belong to a like people, to have a place among a nation of like kind. Hawaii did not make this easy. It offered too much, seemed to affirm too many options. There was no prescribed path, no single style or type that stood out. In hotel rooms, along with the Gideon Bible, guests were often surprised to find both the Book of Mormon and the Teachings of the Buddha. Every ethnic and religious option was represented on the streets of Honolulu. Even at Punahou, the clocks in the library showed the times in Third World nations, an attempt by the administration to reinforce its message of multiculturalism. None of this made it easy for Barack to single out his unique place in the world.

During his years at Punahou, he tried on personas as another man might try on clothes. Was he the angry radical brother or

During his years at Punahou, he tried on personas as another man might try on clothes. Was he the angry radical brother or the educated, upwardly mobile black? Was he intent upon destroying the system or rising within it?

the educated, upwardly mobile black? Was he intent upon destroying the system or rising within it? Should he drift in bitterness into drugs and parties—and gripe sessions where he poured out his excuses for failure—or should he nurse an "I'll show them" rage and take on the world? Was it denying his blackness to date a white girl or running from his white world to socialize only with blacks? More vitally, was he fully any one thing in the world? White? Black? American? He wasn't sure. He read Baldwin, Ellison, Hughes, Wright, and DuBois, but found no map for the country he sought. All of them ended, he concluded, "exhausted, bitter men, the devil at their heels."[13]

Graduating from Punahou in 1979, he attended Occidental University in Los Angeles for two years but found himself sinking into the aimlessness of some of his friends. He knew he had to pull himself out of the bog. He decided to transfer to Columbia University in New York, and there followed what he later described as a "fundamental rupture in my life." He had not come to a grand plan and certainly had no political ambitions. Yet he did decide that he wanted to, as he put it, "make my mark," that he yearned to be noticed, to do something important—perhaps even to live an exceptional life.[14] He became more serious about his future but was still aware that he had "no guide that might show [him] how to join this troubled world." When he slipped into the back pew of New York's Abyssinian Baptist Church one Sunday and felt the sweet sorrow in an ancient song, he was void of the faith that gave the song wings. He belonged there and didn't, much as it was for him in the world. He was, as his sister, Maya, would later say, walking "between worlds."[15]

The truth is he was lonely. By the time he finished college with a degree in political science in 1983, he was living half a world away from his only family. His father, whom he had not seen in more than a decade, had recently died. It is possible that having learned detachment from his anthropologist mother, he had made detachment a lifestyle. He was in a self-imposed prison, one created by both his need and his curse to look upon the world as though he were not a part of it. He became a rootless wanderer and was haunted by "the mixed blood, the divided soul, the ghostly image of the tragic mulatto trapped between two worlds."[16]

This was his state when he landed in Chicago in 1985. He had recently tasted work in the New York corporate world and found it thin. Arriving in a city he barely knew, he went to work for a social improvement organization called Developing Communities Project. His Herculean task was to mobilize people on Chicago's South Side to make positive change in their community. His world now became the roiling, largely black, deeply frustrated, poverty-ridden yet often joyful streets of the neighborhoods that gave the world both the music of Muddy Waters and the fiction of Upton Sinclair. Obama gave himself to any cause important to the people—from asbestos to crime, from church unity to prostitution—as a means of building consensus and thus political power. He spent many of his days interviewing people about their needs and complaints. He called meetings, cajoled, endured repeated humiliation, and enjoyed minor victories. He was ambitious and came to see the connection between crisis and power. As he wrote later in *Dreams from My Father*, "Issues, action, power, self-interest. I liked these concepts. They bespoke a certain hardheadedness, a worldly lack of sentiment; politics, not religion."[17]

> In the community, people wanted to know where he got his faith before they wanted to hear his ideas for social improvement. But he had no faith, not in the religious sense.

Yet religion became his crisis, personally and professionally. He admitted to coworkers that he was "not very religious" and was told that this only put a barrier between himself and the people. In the community, people wanted to know where he got his faith before they wanted to hear his ideas for social improvement. But he had no faith, not in the religious sense. His work with pastors hadn't helped that cause. Though he found some clergymen who were willing to roll up their sleeves and work to heal the community, many pastors he met were either politicians with clerical collars or men who were too tradition-bound to be of any use—or to offer any refreshment to his parched soul.

He was also pressing against the limits of his mother's worldview, and it was a disturbing experience.

I had no community or shared traditions in which to ground my most deeply held beliefs. The Christians with whom I worked recognized themselves in me; they saw that I knew their Book and shared their values and sang their songs. But they sensed that a part of me remained removed, *detached*, an observer among them. I came to realize that without a vessel for my beliefs, without an unequivocal commitment to a particular community of faith, I would be consigned at some level to always remain apart, free in the way that my mother was free, but also alone in the same ways she was ultimately alone.[18]

Ann had loved him, imparted to him a sense of the power of his gifts, and cheered him on as he rose in the world. Much of what he became was due to her devotion. Yet she could not give him what she did not have. As a woman who had rejected faith and looked upon human society much as a scientist looks at cells through a microscope, she paid the price for her detachment by ultimately having no belonging, no tribe, no people to claim for her own. Though she could be a warm and broadly spiritual person, she was isolated by the detachment she prized. Her legacy might have been his own had he not come to realize the horrible price of her beliefs.

It was as these thoughts troubled his mind that Barack Obama landed in a pew at the 8:00 a.m. Sunday service of Trinity United Church of Christ. He had met some weeks before with the pastor, Jeremiah Wright, though the topic of the discussion had been the community and how Trinity was often perceived by other churches. Obama had a dual agenda. He listened respectfully as Wright talked, but he was also scanning the spirit of the man and testing the waters in light of a change he was considering. The meeting ended, Obama grabbed some material about the church at the front office as he left, and then he let weeks go by.

He was wrestling—with his conscience, his cynicism, his intellectual approach to faith. Asked if he would join a friend at church, he demurred.

> And I would shrug and play the question off, unable to confess that I could no longer distinguish between faith and mere folly, between faith and simple endurance; that while I believed in the sincerity I heard in their voices, I remained a reluctant skeptic, doubtful of my own motives, wary of expedient conversion, having too many quarrels with God to accept a salvation too easily won.[19]

Nevertheless, questions raging and doubts unresolved, he came. As he sat in that Trinity pew early that Sunday morning, he settled into the comforting mercies of the African American church. He knew that this church, like most of its kind, had long ministered to the community as it did to the man, that individual salvation and collective salvation were both noble goals of the black gospel. This idea pleased him. He also felt peace at the notion that in the black church "the lines between sinner and saved were more fluid," that "you needed to embrace Christ precisely because you had sins to wash away" and not because you walked in the door perfect as a glowing gift for God.[20] This he needed to know as he sat there, a man in doubt and conflict.

The sermon that day was on a topic that would live in his soul and in his politics. It was called "The Audacity of Hope." In the skilled rhetorical hands of Jeremiah Wright, the lesson mounted into a grand symphony of uniquely African American preaching. Searing biblical content was overlaid against social commentary and all brought to bear on the sufferings and promised victories of each individual life in the congregation. Somehow, beginning with the slender hopes of Hannah, the mother of the prophet Samuel, Wright managed to reflect on the injustices of Sharpsville and Hiroshima, the follies of state and federal government in America, and the callousness of the middle class. Despite the broad range of references, or perhaps because of them, a laser of hope penetrated Barack's soul. At sermon's end, he found himself in tears.

It was a beginning. The process that followed took months and could not be hurried. And when the turning came, it was not attended by angels and flashes of light. In the retelling it did not have the ring of the famous conversions of history, with their great moral transformations and dramatic encounters with God. Instead, it was a decision to enter a faith by joining a people of faith, to come home to a community and so come home to God. Indeed, as Obama has explained, "It came about as a choice and not an epiphany; the questions I had did not magically disappear. But kneeling beneath that cross on the South Side of Chicago, I felt God's spirit beckoning me. I submitted myself to His will and dedicated myself to discovering His truth."[21]

2

My House, Too

PRESIDENTIAL CANDIDATE SAM BROWNBACK WAS FEELING relieved. Appearing with Barack Obama at a 2006 World AIDS Day summit sponsored by Rick Warren's Saddleback Church, Brownback said he felt a bit more "comfortable" than he had the last time the two presidential candidates shared a stage. "We were both addressing the NAACP," he told the crowd of several thousand. "They were very polite to me. I think they kind of wondered, 'Who's this guy from Kansas?' And then Barack Obama follows, and they're going, 'Okay, now we've got Elvis.'"

Assuming that Warren's evangelical church would be home turf for a conservative Roman Catholic like himself, Brownback then turned to Obama and said, "Welcome to *my* house!" The audience exploded with laughter and applause. A few moments later, though, Obama took the stage and said, "There is one thing I have to say, Sam. This is my house, too. This is God's house."[1]

Once again, Obama showed his skill at intercepting the political long pass. Brownback intended an appeal to his base. Obama wasn't having it. Refusing to yield an inch of the religious high ground, he made it clear to all that not only would he not be moved from his rightful place in the Christian fold, but he also would not allow newcomers to the crisis of AIDS, newcomers like Warren's evangelicals, to forget that Obama's political tribe began addressing that issue long ago. *Be a Christian with me, Sam,* he was saying, *but don't act like my older brother. This is my house, too.*

Though Obama was declaring his membership in the universal house of God, his more local house of faith is far removed from Rick Warren's Saddleback Church and the largely white enclaves of Lake Forest, California. Instead, Obama's spiritual house sits nearly half a continent away, in the heart of housing projects and steel mesh–wrapped businesses on Chicago's black and proud South Side.

A VISITOR TO A SUNDAY MORNING SERVICE AT TRINITY United Church of Christ is first struck by the worshippers who walk the weary streets of their South Side neighborhood en route to their spiritual home. Mothers balance on high heels while wrestling handfuls of fussy children along broken sidewalks; fathers make a game of carrying sweetly dressed daughters on broad shoulders past the never-quiet traffic on West Ninety-fifth Street. Some have walked for miles, yet there is determination in each step born of a spiritual hunger and a universal yearning to assume a place among one's people.

Drawing near to the impressive yellow-beige building that houses Trinity Church, the visitor also senses the care and planning that pervades the life of this spiritual family. Kind but imposing security men are positioned strategically around the building, each dressed stylishly for church but with earbuds and walkie-talkies protruding. Some are armed, as has become the unfortunate need of many large churches around the nation. Stepping from the obviously loved and tenderly maintained grounds through the main doors, the visitor is greeted by older men and women who put the loving face on this carefully crafted system of hospitality.

If the visitor is late, he may well be asked to stand in lines defined by velvet ropes and fastened to brass stands, much as he might see at an upscale movie theater. The message is clear: *This is not just a church; this is a cultural phenomenon, a religious experience of historic importance for the people who attend.* Hundreds throng to enter, sometimes arriving in the still-dark hours of the morning just to get a seat. Don't be late.

Passing through the lobby, the visitor might easily miss the first symbols of the defining vision of this people. A picture of a black Jesus hangs behind an information desk, His arms extended around a black family radiating joy and contentment. There are, too, black faces in the biblical scenes depicted in the glorious stained glass of Trinity Church. These are silent testimony to the theological vision at the heart of this African American family of faith.

While the crowd begins to fill up the nearly twenty-seven hundred seats of the contemporary-style sanctuary, the visitor cannot help but notice the clothing of the worshippers. There are, of course, the brilliant dresses, hats, and fashionable suits one expects of a black church in America. There is also more casual attire—jeans and leather jackets; stepping-out-at-night, low-cut dresses; and even work clothes worn by the city bus driver who did not have time to change. All are welcome. Yet in larger numbers than most black churches can boast, the worshippers at this church dress in the attire of Africa. Dashikis and flowing robes sing their colors in African hues, and huge turbans bound with exotic knots are worn by women who understand the power of the statement they make. One quickly realizes that this is not a fashion show: these are the uniforms of a worldview.

Ushers wearing white gloves seat all comers, while older women keep a mothering eye on the waiting crowd. "Sir, is that a recording device? Oh, your electronic Bible? Okay then, enjoy the service." "Ma'am, we don't allow cameras. May I ask you to put that away until you leave the grounds?" All is done with kindness and grace, yet with the underlying firmness of elders tending their clan.

Indeed, the whole system of gathering has obviously been crafted with an eye to serving the outsider while protecting church members from intrusion. This is, after all, a spiritual family of nearly ten thousand, where a U.S. senator and some of the most famous African Americans in the country sometimes attend. Members of the press are kindly tagged and assigned a handler. Attendees smile knowingly at an unshaven French camera crew in jeans and boots, now escorted by an elegant Nigerian woman in a brilliantly colored gown, explaining what may and may not be done. Reporters who stray off-limits may well be met by mountainous security men, some former members of the Chicago Bears, who gently suggest a return to bounds.

At the exact moment of the published starting time, a woman moves to the pulpit to make announcements. So striking is her manner that years after seeing her for the first time, Barack Obama remembered the "graying hair" and "no-nonsense demeanor." At her first word, the crowd immediately falls to silence. This is a disciplined congregation.

If the visitor does not allow himself to be bored by this ritual of information sharing common to all churches, he may come to understand something of the soul of this people from these few introductory moments. Careful attention over time will reveal that on a budget of nearly $10 million—respectable but not exceptional for a church of its size—Trinity sponsors more than seventy ministries and dozens of educational institutions around the world. There are alcohol and drug-addiction outreaches, ex-offender programs, hospices, counseling services, elder care, and many other social services of nearly every kind. The church has given more than a million dollars to the United

Negro College Fund and has raised hundreds of thousands to support scholarships and schools, some as far away as Africa and the Middle East. There are academic programs, college preparatory services, and even college fairs. Consciously resisting a "silo mentality," in which wealth is stored but not used, Trinity clearly intends to invest wealth to change the culture of its people. It also clearly intends to break from the black church of tradition. Trinity sponsors a large outreach to gay and lesbian singles, an emphasis both unusual and controversial among African American Christians.

Listening a bit more closely, the visitor may come to understand that this is not just a congregation of the downtrodden. There are in attendance multimillionaire businessmen, politicians, medical doctors, and hundreds of teachers and college professors, including at least a dozen from the prestigious University of Chicago. The church is sometimes criticized in its own community for being too "buppie": black, upwardly mobile, professional. This fact does not seem to bother the pastors. Several of them hold degrees from Ivy League schools, and no senior staffer is without an impressive academic résumé.

The announcements completed, the worship begins. Often, it starts in a manner reminiscent of any evangelical megachurch in America: an energetic leader in black jeans and a T-shirt exhorts and shouts for response between lively songs carefully chosen to energize the crowd, drums and bass guitar throbbing. Yet here at Trinity, this continues only for a short while before the choir files in, several hundred strong, and takes the lead.

Choir members are dressed in a loosely coordinated African color scheme, each showing individuality and yet connection to the whole in their dress.

The music now ended, a few prayers are voiced; then a young man takes the pulpit. His name is Rev. Otis Moss III, and he is the new lead pastor. Tall and handsome, he is thirty-seven years old, a Yale graduate, and he comes to Trinity from a successful pastorate in Georgia. His oratorical skills are immediately obvious. He speaks in a warm, clipped style that captures both Ivy League and the street; that is, both college professor and black poet. It is easy to understand why the congregation chose this man to guide them for the decades to come.

His sermon is wrapped around the theme of the crucifixion of Jesus, and it is a masterpiece of exposition and tender narrative. He summons characters from history and gives them personality and voice. Cadence and repetition mount, bringing the crowd to its feet often and driving home the central theme. Scholarship—the dissected New Testament Greek word, the patiently explained custom from the time of Jesus, the carefully chosen historical anecdote—merges with a pastor's insight into human nature to craft an impact on the congregation that is at once educational, inspiring, and of unsparing challenge. Few sermons as good will be preached anywhere in America on this Sunday morning.

The outsider, particularly if he is white, will notice two likely unexpected characteristics of the preaching. The first is the altered detail of Bible stories from what he has known. Jesus is a "half-naked man of color," who loses His life at the conspiring hands of a corrupt white Italian nation and the coconspirators within His own race. Probably, the white visitor has never thought of the crucifixion story in this way. The second feature is how at any moment in the sermon, a Bible story might be shifted to its racial or political parallel today. Trumped-up charges against Jesus at the hands of the Pharisees swiftly become the means of understanding how the Los Angeles police plant evidence or how George W. Bush will likely have to place weapons of mass destruction in Iraq where there were none before. These asides excite the crowd as much as the passionate biblical narrative of the sermon, and the visitor notes that even the few white members of the congregation often stand up in support of these moments of political commentary.

> *Hovering over all is the spirit of a man who is not present, who is only occasionally mentioned, but who nevertheless pervades the whole. His name is Rev. Jeremiah A. Wright Jr., and he has been the senior pastor of this people, until recently, for thirty-six years.*

Hovering over all is the spirit of a man who is not present, who is only occasionally mentioned, but who nevertheless pervades the whole. He is referred to with honor in nearly every prayer. His name, offered as an aside in an announcement, prompts applause. During the sermon, the difficulties he has endured of late are compared with the sufferings of Jesus and His abuse by both the cowardly religious and the sinfully political. When the sermon concludes with an impassioned description of Jesus being lifted up on the cross, this man is also portrayed as one whose sufferings will allow him to be lifted up and vindicated before a watching world.

His name is Rev. Jeremiah A. Wright Jr., and he has been the senior pastor of this people, until recently, for thirty-six years. When he first became their shepherd in 1972, the congregation numbered only eighty-seven souls but had already found the courage to declare themselves "unashamedly black and unapologetically Christian." Ablaze with purpose and with his red-tinged Afro nearly a symbol of his passion, Wright began building in those days what would become a Chicago institution and the largest church of the United Church of Christ denomination.

Now, though, these achievements tend to fade behind the firestorm that has attended the end of his pastoral ministry. For this is the man whose raging statements have been viewed on YouTube hundreds of thousands of times, who has declared that "God damns America," that racism rules the United States—the "U.S.K.K.K.A."—and that the horrors of September 11, 2001, were "America's chickens coming home to roost." And he also is the man who has perhaps become the largest political liability for his spiritual son, Senator Barack Obama.

Ask about the man's character among his congregation, though, and a different picture forms. A deacon recalls when Dr.

Wright spoke at a struggling church nearby and afterward refused his honorarium, insisting that instead the money be used for the church's meager building fund. An older woman recalls traveling to Africa with her pastor and noticing the tears in his eyes as he taught about the motherland of his race. Then there are tales of the tender reminiscences of childhood that fill his sermons, of the pastoral gentleness of his visits to troubled homes, and of his generosity in a poor community.

Older men cackle as they recall Wright's humor—and his strong language. He is known for lacing his sermons with the vocabulary of the street. A visiting minister to Trinity recently found himself at a point in his sermon where he shouted the word "No!" as part of a story. Then, pausing, he said instead, "Hell, no!" With a smile, he explained, "Jeremiah Wright taught me that." The crowd erupted in knowing laughter. Dr. Wright might be a "cussin' preacher," but he's their preacher, and they love him.

Wright was born in 1941 to a Baptist pastor's home in Philadelphia. The son and grandson of ministers, he enrolled as a freshman at the historically black Virginia Union University when he was eighteen. Before he finished his degree, though, he left the school to join the U.S. Marines. Stories vary as to why. The nobler version is that he was inspired by John F. Kennedy's "Ask not what your country can do for you" speech and gave up his student deferment to serve his country. The more likely reason is that he became disenchanted with Christianity's weak support for the civil rights movement and lost interest in a pastoral calling. Whatever the cause, he served in the Second Marine Division and then transferred into the Navy. He returned to college in 1967 when he enrolled in historically black Howard University in Washington DC, earning a bachelor's degree and a master's degree in English.

There was turmoil beneath the surface of this journey. Wright, characteristically, tells the story, sparing nothing. At Virginia Union, he had begun to see "the underside (or the seedy side) of the Black church and hypocritical Black preachers."[2] This disillusionment paralleled the rise of the civil rights movement. Wright participated in sit-ins and resisted "the 'honkies' I was growing to hate with each passing day."[3] Bluntly, he says, "[in those days I] was singing as a soloist in the traveling university choir, getting drunk for the first time in my life, and trying to sort out my call to ministry."[4]

His mentor was Dr. Samuel Proctor, a professor he met at Virginia Union and a leading black educator who served also at North Carolina A&T and Rutgers University. Wright remembers that at the time, Proctor "produced more African American PhDs at Rutgers than any other person in the history of the school."[5] More important for the man Wright would become, "Proctor was always pointing me to a higher calling and a deeper commitment to a faith grounded in a carpenter from Capernaum who knew oppression, who knew hatred and who knew colonialism, but who also knew (personally) a God who was greater than any government and who promised a peace more powerful than any peace the 'world' could ever give."[6]

With Proctor's encouragement, Wright reclaimed his sense of calling to ministry and began to prepare by earning a master's at the University of Chicago Divinity School and later a doctorate at United Theological Seminary.

As he stepped into ministry, he was fully aware of the crisis of faith in the black community. Blacks were leaving the Christian church in the 1970s for other religious traditions that seemed to belong more naturally to the black experience. The Nation of Islam and the Black Hebrew Israelites, among others, thrived as a result. "They didn't know African-American history," Wright insists. "They were leaving churches by the boatloads. The church seemed so disconnected from their struggle for dignity and humanity."[7] About this time Wright accepted the lead role at Trinity United Church of Christ.

He would build at Trinity on the foundation of a new black theology, one that began to emerge in the late 1960s to fierce controversy. Wright would insist, though, that this theology— the Christianity that arises organically from the black experience, that in fact *is* the black experience—did not originate in the 1960s or even in America. It was fashioned, he would preach, in the struggles of the Old Testament people of God and through the birth of a New Testament faith. It was hammered out on the anvil of the transatlantic slave trade and systematized by black thinkers and theologians for generations before finding its public voice in the crises of race that attended the troubled decade of the 1960s in America. It was the theology, he would proclaim, of a people determined to be subjects in history, not objects.

The symbolic call to arms of this black theology may have been sounded on July 31, 1966, when fifty-one black pastors took out a full-page ad in the *New York Times* demanding results in eradicating racism. The age was in turmoil, and the black church was beginning to engage—and engage aggressively. A manifesto issued by a gathering of black theologians in Atlanta three years later ended with Eldridge Cleaver's battle cry: "We shall have our manhood. Or the earth will be leveled by our efforts to gain it." The killing of their leaders and the suffering that plagued their communities were too much to tolerate in silence any longer. Though the black churches came late to the battle for social equality—Martin Luther King Jr. had been kicked out of his denomination just years before for the "excesses" of his political activism—when they finally took up the challenge, they did so with a vengeance.

> *Though the black churches came late to the battle for social equality, when they finally took up the challenge, they did so with a vengeance.*

In 1969, theologian James Cone issued the Magna Carta of black theology, a work called *Black Theology and Black Power*. Influenced by Stokely Carmichael's black power ideology, Malcolm X's intellectual taunts of white Christianity, and Martin Luther King Jr.'s demand for civil rights, Cone built a theology of and for the black experience. At the heart of this theology was the idea of liberation. Since Jesus described Himself as a liberator—whose task was to "preach good news to the poor . . . to proclaim freedom for the prisoners . . . to release the oppressed"[8]—the work of the church now ought to be the same.

This core idea sounds Christian enough, but Cone came to emphasize this matter of liberation nearly to the exclusion of all other biblical doctrines. On the matter of revelation, for example, he maintained that revelation only occurs where God enters history to liberate the oppressed from their oppressors. That was a break from the traditional perspective that God speaks through Scripture, by the Holy Spirit, and through the anointed leaders of His church. Now, with Cone, liberation became both the means and the moment of revelation. "In a word," Cone argued, "God's revelation means liberation—nothing more, nothing less."[9]

Cone also insisted that all who suffer oppression are "black," no matter their skin color. Being black meant taking the side of the oppressed against the oppressor. So when Cone proclaimed that Jesus is black, that whites want Christianity without blackness, and that the Scriptures can be interpreted only by blacks, he was issuing a call to reinterpret Christianity in terms of its lost themes of suffering and liberation, yet he was using language that assured resistance from both white and traditional black churches. In this sense, the black experience became ultimate for Cone:

> I still regard the Bible as an important source of my theological reflections, but not the starting point. The black experience

and the Bible together in dialectical tension serve as my point of departure today and yesterday. The order is significant. I am black first—and everything else comes after that. This means that I read the Bible through the lens of a black tradition of struggle and not as the objective Word of God. The Bible therefore is one witness to God's empowering presence in human affairs, along with other important testimonies.[10]

The corollary is, of course, that whiteness is oppression, that whiteness is slavery, that whiteness is power in opposition to the very thing that Jesus Christ came to do.

Even for those who understood Cone's language—Jesus is a "black" man come to destroy "white" systems of oppression—his message was radical and often violent. A typical sentence from his *A Black Theology of Liberation* reveals the sentiments that enraged white readers and thrilled many black activists: "Black theology must realize that the white Jesus has no place in the black community, and it is our task to destroy him."[11]

> *"Black theology must realize that the white Jesus has no place in the black community, and it is our task to destroy him."*

Similarly, "black theology is concerned only with the tradition of Christianity that is usable in the black liberation struggle."[12] Or, "for too long Christ has been pictured as a blue-eyed honky. Black theologians are right; we need to dehonkify him and thus make him relevant to the black condition."[13] These statements were troubling enough to the society of the day, yet there were others that seemed designed to set a match, almost literally, to the tinderbox of animosity: "The black experience is the feeling one has when attacking the enemy of black humanity by throwing a Molotov cocktail into a white-owned building and watching it go up in flames. We know, of course, that getting rid of evil takes something more than burning down buildings, but one must start somewhere."[14]

In the eyes of most traditional churches, both black and white, Cone was simply mixing Christianity with Marxism. He was remaking Jesus into a "People's Messiah" who preached a message of political liberation rather than spiritual regeneration. Accordingly, some feared, a black man might shoot a white man or burn down a white-owned business and believe himself to be doing the will of Jesus Christ, the Prince of Peace. The same Jesus who told His disciples not only to love all nations but also to teach them to do His will was being presented as a "whitey-hating" black man come to destroy all but black society. Evangelical scholar Francis Schaeffer had written that "liberalism is nothing more than humanism in theological clothing," leading Cone's evangelical critics to conclude that black theology was little more than black bigotry reworking the mission of Jesus.

Radical or not, violent or not, Cone's vision launched a generation of black ministers, and Jeremiah Wright was among them. He became an expert in black theology, not only as Cone taught it but also as other theologians rearticulated and extended it. Taking the lead at Trinity United Church of Christ in 1972, just as black theology was filling its sails with the winds of the age, Wright began preaching his theology of liberation to the oppressed people on Chicago's South Side. It was refreshing to their souls: a strengthening of their hopes in God, a confirmation of their political suspicions, a celebration of their history, an affirmation of the goodness of their race, and an arming for the cultural battles to come.

Through the years, the people of Trinity Church were exposed to a view of the United States far different not only from that taught in the nation's schools, but also from that preached to most black congregations and in most suburban churches of the country. For black people—both black in skin color and "black" as the oppressed—American history as Wright taught it was no longer a noble tale of the advancement of freedom. White Americans might get misty-eyed at the remembrance of Jamestown as the first permanent English settlement on the shores of the New World, but for blacks, Jamestown was where American slavery began in 1619. White Americans could boast of their intrepid founding fathers, but blacks at Trinity Church were urged to remember a compromising generation who spoke movingly of human equality yet who extended slavery. Let politicians tell lies about the glories of America's world wars, Wright would insist, but blacks should recall Jim Crow laws and a segregated army that only begrudgingly tolerated the black flying aces of Tuskegee. Having determined to see the world in terms of the oppressors and the oppressed, Wright found America on the oppressor side almost every time.

Black theology shaped Wright's understanding of the world and America's role in it. The U.S. bombings of Hiroshima and Nagasaki were never bold, ingenious ends to a bloody war. They were massacres of a people of color by a white nation. America's support for Israel? No less than white imperialists oppressing a Palestinian people of color through a client state. America's post-9/11 war in Afghanistan

> Black theology shaped Wright's understanding of the world and America's role in it.

and Iraq? Merely a tyrannical nation sending her people of color to colonize yet another people of color for little more than oil. So it would be with South Africa, Grenada, Native Americans, women, Bosnia, Somalia, Vietnam, gays, lesbians, and immigrants. Jesus came to liberate the downtrodden, and Jeremiah Wright would be His disciple, supporting the oppressed wherever they were to be found in the world.

His views set him in tension not only with many in white America but even with some of his fellow black churchmen. He stood for abortion rights, against school prayer, and for laws protecting gays and lesbians. He urged the U.S. government to pay reparations to blacks for slavery and to pour more foreign aid into Africa. He raged against the "prosperity gospel" of black and white churches and thought nothing of accusing a fellow pastor of promoting a "pimp theology for a prostituted church." His views flew hard and fast on the wings of his astonishing oratorical gifts, and he was not afraid to depart from any text in any sermon to expound on the evils of his society or his race.

Often of surprise to white observers, Wright did not simply wait for the U.S. government to fund the liberation of his people. Indeed, the notorious sermon in which he proclaimed that "God damns America" was titled "Confusing God and Government," a call to cease looking to government to fulfill the promises of God. Wright was not waiting for a government check. During his years at Trinity, he preached the values of black self-sufficiency and, despite his pastoral load, helped start corporations to bring prosperity to the people in his community. He also raged against the insular values of a black middle class, of a people who had just enough to inoculate them against concern for others. He challenged both the wealthy and the poor of his congregation to give—and give radically—for the cause of Jesus in the world.

This, then, was Jeremiah Wright: brilliant, angry, successful, and unapologetic—passionate for his people, passionate for his Christ, and passionate to understand the world in exclusively liberation terms. And his critics raged. He was a "demonized man," "anti-Semitic," "a Communist fellow traveler," and "a racist." He was perceived to be the epitome of the problem with black leadership in America, a cult leader of heretical views.

Yet while his critics spewed, his influence and following

grew. There seemed to be no middle ground in public opinion. Jeremiah Wright was either demon or deliverer.

> *There seemed to be no middle ground in public opinion. Jeremiah Wright was either demon or deliverer. The truth is that he was, and is, a conundrum, hard to reconcile, a mixture of greatness and grief.*

The truth is that he was, and is, a conundrum, hard to reconcile, a mixture of greatness and grief. He could lead thousands to faith and then spout urban myth as gospel. He could proclaim the "old, old story" of Christian truth and the latest conspiracy theories in nearly the same breath. He could bitterly rail against his nation and yet be, as he was, the most respected black preacher of spiritual revival in the country. He could lead a people to holiness and swear like a gangbanger in the pulpit. He could be generous and small, ennobling and crushing, glorious and dark.

Then there were stories like this one that only deepened the mystery. William A. Von Hoene Jr. was a white man in love with a black woman. She was a member of Trinity Church and an activist in the cause of her people. She was also in love with William—and deeply troubled by it. How could she marry a white man and keep respect in her black community? Wouldn't a white husband undermine all she hoped to accomplish for her race? So in her torment, she broke off her engagement to William.

Jeremiah Wright heard about her crisis. He called her, asked her to "drop everything" to meet with him, and then spent four hours pouring out his heart. God does not want us to make decisions about people based on race, he told her. The future belongs to those who are prepared to break down barriers. Racial divisions aren't acceptable, no matter the pain that caused them. Marry this man, he told her, and forge a new history together. And a few months later, Rev. Jeremiah Wright performed the ceremony in which the white William married his African American bride.[15]

This from the racist pastor of Trinity United Church of Christ. This from the man who damns America in the name of God. This from the scholar who claims that Jesus is black. And all of this, the angry and the kind, the holy and the harsh, would come to bear on the life of Barack Obama.

THE SUNDAY MORNING SERVICE AT TRINITY UNITED Church of Christ has dismissed, and the visitor makes his way to the door. Walking out into the biting Chicago air, he falls in with the departing crowd to greetings exchanged through scarves and gloved hands.

The visitor finds himself behind a mother and her son. He has seen these two earlier that morning walking their half mile to church against the cold.

"Momma, do you wanna hear what I learned this morning?"

"Yes, baby. Tell me"

"I learned that the man who helped Jesus carry the cross was from Africa. He was prob'ly black."

"That's right, baby. What else did you learn?"

"Teacher also told us that some of the men at Antioch, where they sent out Paul and *Billabus* to be missionaries, some of those men were black like you and me too."

"It's Barnabas, honey, but that's right. One of those men's names even means 'black man.'"

"That's right, Momma. And did you know that there was an *unchun* from Ethiopia? He's in the Bible and he was black too."

"Baby, you say that word *eunuch*, but you are so right. That man was a black man from Africa. I'm so proud of you knowing that."

"I know, Momma. I can't wait to tell 'em at school. I bet they don't know it."

The visitor, having heard, begins to understand. And though he is white and of another theological stream, he looks back at Trinity United Church of Christ and sees it for a moment through different eyes, and as though for the first time.

3

Faith Fit for the Age

MEN FIND GOD IN VARYING WAYS, EVEN WITHIN THE Christian fold. For most, faith comes in a progression, through a layering of truth over time. Others grasp God in moments of crisis, in desperation, clenching certainties that sustain them all their lives. Then there are those, a select few, who experience dramatic encounters with God, who glimpse with human eyes the glories of an invisible realm. Truly, religious conversions are as varied as those converted and the ways of Providence in dealing with men. There is no single pattern, no schedule by which to compare. It is the destination that remains firm. The road to faith winds and bends.

The conversion of Barack Obama, too, defies pattern, refuses to fall cleanly between theological lines. Yet his turning to faith was one fit for his age. He came as many of his generation do—not so much to join a tradition as to find belonging among a people; not so much to accept a body of doctrine as to find welcome for what they already believe; not so much to surrender their lives but to enhance who they already are.

We should remember how Obama has described his conversion, the phrases that have played so often in his speeches and books. In *The Audacity of Hope*, he wrote that "it came about as a choice and not an epiphany; the questions I had did not magically disappear. But kneeling beneath that cross on the South Side of Chicago, I felt God's spirit beckoning me. I submitted myself to His will, and dedicated myself to discovering His truth."[1] In later interviews he sometimes used more traditional language. He has, he says, a "personal relationship with Jesus Christ," and he believes "in the redemptive death and resurrection of Jesus Christ . . . that faith gives me a path to be cleansed of sin and have eternal life."[2]

At Trinity United Church of Christ, a call to faith, an "altar call," occurs at the end of most every Sunday service. It follows a now-familiar pattern in American religion. The sermon comes to a close and takes the form of an appeal. Jesus is calling, the crowd is told. As music fills the sanctuary, those who believe God is dealing with them are called to the front. Don't hesitate, the pastor urges; this is about God and you. Forget the crowd, the cameras. Your friends and family will wait. Come do the business your soul yearns to do. Soon, individuals rise from the crowd and make their way to the front. The Trinity staff is prepared for this moment. Ushers walk the aisles, urging the willing to the fore. There, all are greeted by leaders who form the sometimes weeping seekers into a line. The pastor gives gentle words of instruction and offers a prayer for each soul. Then all are moved to another room for counsel. As they go, the congregation applauds and shouts words of support. Many in the crowd have walked that tearful line before.

Obama has recounted that he first met with Jeremiah Wright and then attended Trinity Church in 1985. Before long he heard the transforming "Audacity of Hope" sermon. Yet it was months before he responded to a call to faith, months before he made his way to the front of the room and confessed his faith in Christ. He was likely battling his lifestyle of detachment. It would have been more natural for him to sit and watch but feel himself apart, to protect his heart through distance. The power of Trinity Church wouldn't allow it, though. Then, too, he "felt God's spirit beckoning."[3]

> *He heard the transforming "Audacity of Hope" sermon. Yet it was months before he responded to a call to faith, months before he made his way to the front of the room and confessed his faith in Christ.*

The day came, and when it did, Obama rose after a particularly powerful sermon and made his way to the front, likely with a white-gloved usher at his side. He would have stood in a line and received a prayer and instruction. If he was willing, he would have made his way to a side room where fathers in faith would have helped him find his God.

In early retellings of this story, before the phrases were honed into the literature now so well known, Obama says that while at the front of the church, "I did not fall out."[4] The phrase has likely been dropped because it is too esoteric, too much a part of the black and Pentecostal experience for most Americans to understand. But to "fall out" means to be so overcome by the power of God or conviction that one can no longer stand and thus falls to the ground. When people at Trinity fall out, ministers usually attend them, pray for them while they are prostrate, and then help the groggy converts to their feet after they "come to." Obama would have seen this repeatedly in the months he had attended Trinity. It might have given him pause, made him hesitate in responding before he did. This "falling out" might have been something he hoped to avoid, something he was too self-conscious, too Columbia University, to want to do. But on the day when he risked it to grasp his new faith, the experience did not occur. Perhaps he was relieved.

Critics of Obama and, certainly, of Jeremiah Wright wonder whether anything approximating the traditional Christian gospel is preached at Trinity Church. Wright's political pronouncements have been so radical and his demeanor in YouTube clips so angry that it is hard for some, particularly evangelicals, to accept that the church is anything more than a black Marxist recruitment center. Yet this is part of the sometimes confusing nature of both Wright and his church. Yes, Jesus Christ is offered to sinners as the Son of God who died and rose again. Yes, the church calls men to be saved from death and hell through confessing their wrongs and submitting their lives to a crucified Christ. Yes, this is the "born-again, new birth, blood-washed, Spirit-empowered Christianity" that evangelicals know.

Exactly what Barack Obama experienced and what he understood at the time of his conversion is hard to discern. He did not use the language of the traditional convert to Christianity to describe his experience. He is the product of a new, postmodern generation that picks and chooses its own truth from traditional faith, much as a man customizes his meal at a buffet. Obama does not recount that he felt an emptiness in his soul, was burdened by the weight of his sins, and so responded to the love of Jesus, who promised to save him and remake him in the image of God. This is the language of evangelicalism. He says, instead, that he was seeking a "vessel" for his values, a "community or shared traditions in which to ground my most deeply held beliefs."[5] Rather than yield his mind unreservedly to Scripture and its revelation of God, Obama was relieved that a "religious commitment did not require me to suspend critical thinking."[6] Rather than "renounce the world and its ways"—standard Christian language for breaking with the sinful ways of society—he was pleased that his faith would not require "retreat from the world that I knew and loved."[7] Rather than commit to Jesus Christ because of truth he had already found sure, Obama instead admitted, "[The] questions I had didn't magically disappear," and so in conversion he "dedicated [himself] to discovering [God's] truth."[8]

It was language sure to raise doubts. In an age in which a man can easily lose a political race for lack of religious fluency, Obama risked such broad language in describing his conversion that he pleased only those who preferred the matter remain unresolved. Evangelicals were unimpressed. Young postmodernists rejoiced in the mood of spiritual seeking and the ring of honesty in Obama's words. The language was so broad that even the nonreligious weren't offended. Consider John K. Wilson's understanding of Obama's Christ in *Barack Obama: This Improbable Quest*: "For Obama, Jesus isn't a magical creature to be worshipped blindly; he's a real person to be imitated for his moral example. What's important to Obama about Jesus is not the 'Night of the Living Dead' aspects of a Christian belief in a resurrection, but the moral lessons about self-sacrifice for a larger cause."[9] Though this is far from the Christ of Trinity Church, and from what Obama has described in interviews, the portrayal of his conversion in *The Audacity of Hope* is so broad that it does admit such a view.

The uncertainty that Obama's words inspired was likely intentional. Though it does not appear that he meant to confuse, he did speak with a thoughtful lack of clarity, or perhaps with well-considered doubt, for doubt was—in the first seasons of his Christian life—at the heart of Obama's religion. Indeed, it is not going too far to say that for Obama the young believer, doubt was understood as a form of worship. "I think that religion at its best comes with a big dose of doubt," he once explained.[10] His religion was "a faith that admits doubt, and uncertainty, and mystery. Because, ultimately," he observed, "I think that's how most people understand their faith. In fact, it's not faith if you're absolutely certain. There's a leap that we all take, and when you admit that doubt publicly, it's a form of testimony."[11] This studied uncertainty permeated all of Obama's early faith: "There are aspects of the Christian tradition that I'm comfortable with and aspects that I'm not. There are passages of the Bible that make perfect sense to me and others that I go, 'Ya know, I'm not sure about that.'"[12]

> *"It's not faith if you're absolutely certain. There's a leap that we all take, and when you admit that doubt publicly, it's a form of testimony."*

Making the nature of Obama's early Christian commitment even more difficult to pin down is the way he spoke of other religions. In a speech that included the now famous lines about his conversion—"beneath the cross on the South Side"—he then exulted, "That's a path that has been shared by millions upon millions of Americans—evangelicals, Catholics, Protestants, Jews and Muslims alike; some since birth, others at certain turning points in their lives."[13] It was a statement guaranteed to raise questions about his Christianity. Jews and Muslims don't have evangelical conversion experiences. Undoubtedly, Obama was trying to say that he had found faith on the South Side of Chicago much as people of other faiths were either born into or eventually discovered the meaning of their own religion. Yet by comparing his conversion to the embracing of non-Christian religions, Obama once again blurred the lines of definition, leaving uncertainty about how he viewed his faith.

This line in his speech was more than an unguarded sentence. Obama clearly believed that the form of Christianity he committed to at Trinity Church in 1985 is not the only path to God. "I am rooted in the Christian tradition," he has said. Nevertheless, he has also asserted, "I believe that there are many paths to the same place and that is a belief that there is a higher power, a belief that we are connected as a people."[14] He first saw this broad embrace of the world's faiths modeled by his mother. "In our household," he has explained, "The Bible, [t]he Koran, and the Bhagavad Gita sat on the shelf alongside books of Greek and Norse and African mythology. On Easter or Christmas Day my mother might drag me to church, just as she dragged me to the Buddhist temple, the Chinese New Year celebration, the Shinto shrine, and ancient Hawaiian burial sites."[15] What his mother sought to embed in him was her view that "underlying these religions was a common set of beliefs about how you treat other people and how you aspire to act, not just for yourself, but also for the greater good." Thus, for Obama, Christianity is but one religious tree rooted in the common ethical soil of all human experience.

This foundation of doubt and a Christianity taken as but one of many paths to God overlaid even his most casual discussions of faith in the years before he ascended to the presidency. Every statement seemed a mixture, not only in the sense that it departed from traditional language, but in that there was a joining of disparate themes. Asked by a reporter about his prayer life, Obama spoke of "an ongoing conversation with God," but then hinted that this conversation was actually with himself: "I'm constantly asking myself questions about what I'm doing, why I am doing it."[16] Such an answer admits wide interpretation. Wilson, for example, insists that Obama's prayer life "is not a delusional belief that a supernatural being is talking directly to him. Instead, Obama uses God as a way to check his own ego. He uses prayer to 'take stock' of himself and maintain his 'moral compass.'"[17] Members of Obama's church might be surprised by this conclusion, but Wilson's view is again understandable given the expansive language Obama has used in describing his early spirituality.

This murkiness extended even to Obama's view of the afterlife. When his daughter once asked him about what happens after death—"I don't want to die, Daddy," he recalls her saying—he was unable to assure her about heaven: "I wondered if I should have told her the truth, that I wasn't sure what happens when we die, any more than I was sure of where the soul resides or what existed before the Big Bang."[18] He also wasn't sure about the traditional view of eternal punishment: "I find it hard to believe that my God would consign four-fifths of the world to hell."[19] This leads Wilson to conclude that the "afterlife is neither believed nor disbelieved by Obama; it's ignored because it's an unknowable factor that shouldn't affect what we do on earth."[20]

This view, of course, was deeply disturbing to more traditional, orthodox Christians, for certainty about an afterlife is one of the cardinal doctrines of Christianity, regarded by believers as one of the chief blessings of faith in Jesus Christ. Obama's own church lists heaven among the benefits of salvation in the altar calls that close its services. This is not merely the insistence of evangelicals; it is a central truth of the New Testament. Here too, though, in his view of the Bible, there was evidence of Obama's postmodern picking and choosing. Asked by a reporter how he could so warmly embrace non-Christian faiths when Jesus Christ said, "I am the way, the truth and the life. No one comes to the Father but by me," Obama insisted that this is only a "particular verse" and that its meaning depends on how the few words were interpreted.[21] Similarly, in his support of civil unions for homosexuals, he was not "willing to accept a reading of the Bible that considers an obscure line in Romans to be more defining of Christianity than the Sermon on the Mount."[22] Such statements rankled defenders of traditional Christianity, though, for the Bible itself claims that all its words are "given by inspiration of God" and are "profitable for doctrine."[23] Historically, Christians have believed that no one verse can be set against another to prove it untrue.

What did Barack Obama become, then, on that Sunday morning in 1985? He became, he has often said, a Christian. He confessed his faith in Jesus Christ as the Son of God who died for his sins and rose again. Yet he denied in the years after his conversion that Christianity is the sole path to God, and he applied a great deal of doubt to the doctrines of his faith: the inspiration of Scripture, the matter of the afterlife, the moral standards of tradition. In this he was not alone. His early version of Christianity is shared by most of the mainline Protestant denominations today as well as the unchurched young in America, who routinely rework traditional faith into their generational image.

> *His early version of Christianity is shared by most of the mainline Protestant denominations today as well as the unchurched young in America, who routinely rework traditional faith into their generational image.*

We should draw conclusions cautiously, though. All faith is a work in progress, and no man can be accurately portrayed by a portrait frozen in time. At the very heart of Obama's belief has always been a "Living Word of God" that ever reveals and expands, that comes from unexpected sources. As he wrote in *The Audacity of Hope*, "When I read the Bible, I do so with the belief that it is not a static text but the Living Word and that I must be continually open to new revelations—whether they come from a lesbian friend or a doctor opposed to abortion."[24] If there was anything certain about

Obama's early faith, it was that there would come an unfolding, an evolving, a gradual but certain transformation. Given his faith in a "Living Word," it is natural that "revelation" would come and from the most uncommon and unlikely sources.

And indeed that transformation, that unfolding revelation did come, as we shall see, for religiously Barack Obama is not now what he was in his early Christian days—as certainly as he is not now what he was the day before that transforming Chicago Sunday in 1985.

THE MOST PRESSING CONCERN FOR MOST AMERICANS, though, is not so much Obama's postmodern Christianity but his more than two decades at Trinity United Church of Christ. The images live too vividly in the popular mind to ignore. Jeremiah Wright's heated exchange with Sean Hannity of Fox News. The sermon in which America is damned for her racism. The insistence that HIV/AIDS is a weapon devised by the U.S. government to be used against blacks. The claim that America is an oppressive empire not unlike ancient Rome. The unswerving support for the Palestinian cause. The declaration that the sufferings of September 11, 2001, are the fruits of America's national sins, of her chickens coming home to roost.

That Jeremiah Wright, noted African American leader, holds these views is offensive enough to many Americans. That Barack Obama, now our 44th president, felt comfortable sitting under his ministry for two decades is even more troubling, if polls are to be believed. The critical question, then, is why did Obama stay, not just for some twenty years, but even after his pastor's radical views became public?

He has admitted that his first forays into the world of Trinity were pragmatic. Friends told him that his work in the South Side community would go better if people saw him in church, if they knew where he got his faith. Obama took this as true. It also could not have escaped his notice that attending Trinity was a wise political move. A big, visible church where many upwardly mobile and politically active blacks attended was just the place he wanted to be. He did not deceive himself about this motive for attending church, nor did he fail to admit to it later in life.

Yet once he began to visit the church, all the evidence indicates that he was genuinely captured by the experience. It is significant that, years later, when his connection to Trinity came into question, Obama listed among his reasons for staying that "Rev. Wright preached the gospel of Jesus."[25] It may have been, in part, just that simple. He had come to Trinity with a restless heart, yearning for what the skepticism and the atheism of his upbringing could not provide. Wright's more strident pronouncements aside, the compassion and mercies of Jesus Christ were tenderly preached in Obama's hearing. He would be assured that Jesus, ever the Liberator, was first the Savior who called men to acknowledge Him as God and to welcome His sacrifice for sin. In time, Obama would make this Savior his own. Thus, he would confirm the truth of Saint Augustine, an African church father of the fourth century, who once wrote, "You have formed us for yourself, and our hearts are restless till they find their rest in you." Obama had found the answer for his soul's need, and only a cynical heart would refuse the possibility of a lonely black man in his twenties finding faith through the preaching of God's Word.

At Trinity he also found affirmation and celebration of his African heritage. His exotic background had long been a source of conflict for him. He knew few who were like him and spent much of his youth explaining how he was African, but not really African American, and how he wasn't really either one because his mother was white. Trinity brought an end to the struggle. Each Sunday—in the dress of his fellow church members, in the Pan-African flag at the front of the church, in the songs and the sermons that he heard—Africa, land of his father, was honored. Wright led tour groups to Africa almost every year, invited African Christians to preach in Trinity's pulpit, presented the Bible as truth sprung from African soil, and did all he could to bring glowing honor to the motherland of his race. This ennobled Obama, healed him, fine-tuned his sense of himself, and gave him belonging he had seldom known.

There was, too, the political vision of his newfound church. Had Obama attended another church, he might have heard Christianity preached as a retreat from reality, as a spiritual quest divorced from the world. At still another, he might have been urged to merely seek personal prosperity as a sign of God's approval and grace. Instead, he planted himself at Trinity under Jeremiah Wright and found theological sanction for his political liberalism. Remember that as Obama investigated Trinity

Church, he was looking for a "vessel" for values he already had, for "community or shared traditions in which to ground [his] most deeply held beliefs."

He found it. Trinity was activist, politically liberal, and preached a view of Scripture that rooted individual faith in an obligation to change the world. Through the Liberation Theology of Jeremiah Wright, this meant sanction for political views and passions that Obama yearned to connect to a bedrock of faith. That he was pro-choice was clearly the will of God, according to Wright, for it meant he spoke in defense of the rights of women. That he strongly supported a wide separation between church and state served the vision of keeping the oppressor's hands off the pulpits of the land, of keeping "white" religion from grasping the controls of power. That he spoke in the cause of criminals or immigrants or homosexuals or the poor only meant he was following in the footsteps of Jesus, the Liberator, the "black Jesus" who came to destroy the "white Jesus" of the age.

Obama would also find at Trinity encouragement for his intellectual and professional quest. It is not a coincidence that he attended Harvard, practiced law, ran for public office in Illinois, and sought the presidency all after his connection to Trinity began. Trinity called for

> *Trinity called for people to rise, created an environment of learning and achievement, and modeled the pursuit of intellectual excellence.*

people to rise, created an environment of learning and achieve-ment, and modeled the pursuit of intellectual excellence. Another pastor might joke about a seminary being a cemetery and about how believers could "get their learning and lose their burning." Jeremiah Wright, a man with four earned degrees, used, as Obama later wrote, "twenty-five-cent words" with regularity. He hired only well-educated staff, put university professors in charge of Sunday school classes, and worked to send the youth of his church to the most reputable schools in the land. Understanding a single Jeremiah Wright sermon might require knowing something of Middle East history, Greek, Hebrew, the amendments to the U.S. Constitution, the causes of World War II, the politics of the Sudan, and the details of how syphilis is spread. Obama thrived in such an environment. It fueled his intellectual curiosity, answered his theological questions, and honored his intention to rise on the strength of his mind.

As much as any other good that Trinity offered Obama, it gave him a place to belong. Though he came to faith as a man, he carried the soul of a boy who yearned for a father and a tribe to call his own. Trinity answered that need. Jeremiah Wright became his spiritual father, and the church became a bighearted family of a kind he had never known. In approaching the Barack Obama story preoccupied with politics and race, some neglect to understand the simple joys that Trinity offered him. There were hugs and meals and stories to be shared. Wright could wring a laugh from a crowd that would live for weeks, and no one enjoyed it more than Obama. There were small-group gatherings, basketball games, and meals to be carried to the sick. There were also holy rituals to mark the times of life and sacred ceremonies to define the seasons of the year. Obama put down roots in this welcoming soil. He was baptized and married there. He dedicated his children there and invested his money and his time. He belonged. Indeed, Trinity is the longest-lasting connection of his life, his only spiritual home and arguably the most defining relationship he had ever known before he entered the presidency.

He initially stayed, then. Even after the sermons of Jeremiah Wright embarrassed him and damaged his presidential campaign. When the press was circling and he found himself in the political crossfire because of another man's extremes. He stayed because he had found a faith, a people, the vessel for belief that he had longed for. He stayed because Trinity became the font of his political vision and gave him the religious framing for his sense of professional calling. But there was more, and it helps answer more fully the question that many have been asking: Why didn't he immediately walk away when the firestorm over Wright arose?

He thought about it, and once spoke to another upscale, large church pastor about making a switch. But he stayed because by the time of the crisis, he had more than two decades of history at Trinity, and belonging to a people had become everything to him. He stayed because he had seen his daughters grow up as proud granddaughters of Africa, something he knew another church might not help them do. He stayed because he had learned to "eat the chicken and spit out the bones," to listen to a sermon carefully and distinguish between the revelation of God and the personality of a man. He stayed because you don't abandon family; you can't leave your spiritual father by the side of the road for the varmints and the thieves. He stayed, too, because he largely agreed with Wright—not with the high-flying, angry rhetoric but with the underlying cause of blacks in the world and the righteous work of setting the oppressed free. And he stayed because, as he said in his speech explaining it all to an unforgiving world, "I can no more disown him than I can disown the black community." What more could he do? This was his father. This was his tribe. How could he walk away?

And yet the day of separation came. It came because Wright made it clear he cared more about the cause of black theology than the political aspirations of his spiritual son. It came because Wright seemed to delight in provoking the press with his antics, his much-ridiculed National Press Club speech on April 28, 2008, a prime example. It came because during the heated battles of Obama's presidential campaign even guest speakers at Trinity, like Roman Catholic priest Father Michael Phleger, strutted and spouted political venom. And it came, surely, because Obama could see his political opponents coming for him and knew his association with Trinity and Wright would be ground zero for a right wing attack. And when it came, it came with sadness, with grief for the loss of years and the pain that politics presses into private life. But it came, nonetheless, this separation, leaving a void and a wound that likely will never fully leave the life of Barack Obama.

To his credit, Obama tried to turn this hurtful, humiliating episode in a redemptive direction with his "A More Perfect Union" speech, surely one of the finest of his life. If he could not keep his spiritual journey from the front pages of America's newspapers, he would use the opportunity to heal what had been torn in the nation's life and to perhaps improve his political fortunes in the process.

> *If he could not keep his spiritual journey from the front pages of America's newspapers, he would use the opportunity to heal what had been torn in the nation's life and to perhaps improve his political fortunes in the process.*

Given on March 18, 2008, at Philadelphia's National Constitution Center, the speech was an attempt not only to explain Obama's ties to Jeremiah Wright and Trinity United Church of Christ, but also to help America understand the meaning of the black church experience. First, though, Obama had to show that he understood the anger and the offense:

I have already condemned, in unequivocal terms, the statements of Reverend Wright that have caused such controversy. For some, nagging questions remain. Did I know him to be an occasionally fierce critic of American domestic and foreign policy? Of course.

Did I ever hear him make remarks that could be considered controversial while I sat in church? Yes. Did I strongly disagree with many of his political views? Absolutely—just as I'm sure many of you have heard remarks from your pastors, priests, or rabbis with which you strongly disagreed.

Yet, he would not allow this controversy to be seen simply as a difference of opinion between pastor and parishioner. Something deeper, more profound was at stake:

But the remarks that have caused this recent firestorm weren't simply controversial. They weren't simply a religious leader's effort to speak out against perceived injustice. Instead, they expressed a profoundly distorted view of this country—a view that sees white racism as endemic, and that elevates what is wrong with America above all that we know is right with America; a view that sees the conflicts in the Middle East as rooted primarily in the actions of stalwart allies like Israel, instead of emanating from the perverse and hateful ideologies of radical Islam.

As such, Reverend Wright's comments were not only wrong but divisive, divisive at a time when we need unity; racially charged at a time when we need to come together to solve a set of monumental problems—two wars, a terrorist threat, a falling economy, a chronic health care crisis, and potentially devastating climate change—problems that are neither black or white or Latino or Asian, but rather problems that confront us all.

Still, Obama wanted America to understand, wanted to help the nation see why he would stay at a church when he often disagreed with the pastor:

> Why associate myself with Reverend Wright in the first place, they may ask? Why not join another church? And I confess that if all that I knew of Reverend Wright were the snippets of those sermons that have run in an endless loop on the television and YouTube, or if Trinity United Church of Christ conformed to the caricatures being peddled by some commentators, there is no doubt that I would react in much the same way.
>
> But the truth is, that isn't all that I know of the man. The man I met more than twenty years ago is a man who helped introduce me to my Christian faith, a man who spoke to me about our obligations to love one another; to care for the sick and lift up the poor. He is a man who served his country as a U.S. Marine; who has studied and lectured at some of the finest universities and seminaries in the country, and who for over thirty years led a church that serves the community by doing God's work here on Earth—by housing the homeless, ministering to the needy, providing day care services and scholarships and prison ministries, and reaching out to those suffering from HIV/AIDS.

Then, in almost pleading terms, Obama called his listeners to understand that the black church is not like other churches. It isn't just something you join or become a member of in the lightest terms. It is something you become woven into, something that fashions you so thoroughly that you can barely understand yourself apart from it:

> Like other predominantly black churches across the country, Trinity embodies the black community in its entirety—the doctor and the welfare mom, the model student and the former gang-banger. Like other black churches, Trinity's services are full of raucous laughter and sometimes bawdy humor. They are full of dancing, clapping, screaming, and shouting that may seem jarring to the untrained ear. The church contains in full the kindness and cruelty, the fierce intelligence and the shocking ignorance, the struggles and successes, the love and yes, the bitterness and bias that make up the black experience in America.
>
> And this helps explain, perhaps, my relationship with Reverend Wright. As imperfect as he may be, he has been like family to me. He strengthened my faith, officiated my wedding, and baptized my children. Not once in my conversations with him have I heard him talk about any ethnic group in derogatory terms, or treat whites with whom he interacted with anything but courtesy and respect. He contains within him the contradictions—the good and the bad—of the community that he has served diligently for so many years. I can no more disown him than I can disown the black community.

The thirty-seven-minute speech achieved its purpose. The nation began discussing race in the raw, transparent terms natural to a younger generation. The uniqueness of the black church became an eagerly debated topic from seminaries to television talk shows. And Barack Obama's bid for the presidency became more popular than ever according to every leading poll. Even conservative fire breather Newt Gingrich called the speech "brave."

More important, though, was what the speech revealed of Obama's soul. Now, tried by political fire and religious onslaught, he was no longer the "tragic mulatto trapped between two worlds," as he had once written of himself. He was no longer the rootless wanderer without place and without belonging, gazing with detachment at believers in a faith he did not share. No, now he belonged. He knew who he was. He was a black man. He was a Christian. He belonged to the black church. And he was an American, a man who loved his country and knew she could be better still, particularly for her people of color.

> *He knew who he was. He was a black man. He was a Christian. He belonged to the black church. And he was an American, a man who loved his country and knew she could be better still, particularly for her people of color.*

Yet we should keep in mind that neither Obama's conversion nor his years at Trinity would be of such importance were it not for his belief that faith ought to influence governance, that religion has a legitimate role in the marketplace of political ideas. This is not only significant as a break from the traditional secularism of the political Left, but it is critical given the unique religious values Obama has carried with him into the Oval Office. It is a commitment that has thrust him into heated political battles, forced him into painful soul-searching, and lifted him to the fore of a new style of faith-based politics, as we shall see.

Ann Dunham with her son, Barack. "For all her professed secularism," Obama has written, "my mother was in many ways the most spiritually awakened person that I've ever known."

The joy of ocean waves: Barack in the surf near Honolulu.

Young Barack Obama delights in swinging a baseball bat during his early years in Hawaii.

*A Happy Child: A perpetually smiling Barack reflects
the contentment of his young life in the early 1960s.*

Barack is embraced by his biological father at the Honolulu Airport in the early 1970s. This was the last time Barack ever saw the man whose name he bore.

Barack, his mother, Ann, and his sister, Maya, sit with Lolo Soetoro, who took the family to Indonesia and then taught young Barack his broad, syncretistic form of Islam.

Stanley and Madelyn Dunham embrace a teenage Barack. Their love, their faith, and their idiosyncrasies would lastingly impact his life.

Barack as a student at Columbia University, exploring the glories of New York City.

"We worship an awesome God in the Blue States":
The 2004 Democratic Party Convention speech that started it all.

"I can no more disown him than I can disown the black community":
Barack Obama and the Reverend Jeremiah Wright Jr.

*Natasha and Malia Ann Obama with their parents,
Barack and Michelle.*

*President Barack Obama with First Lady Michelle
and daughters Malia and Natasha (Sasha)*

"I am rooted in the Christian tradition": Barack Obama at prayer.

Barack Obama's "improbable quest" leads to the
Democratic presidential nomination in 2008.

4

The Altars of State

THE CANDIDATE WAS UNDER ATTACK. THE LONG AND bruising campaign had worn away all civility, and the heavy bombardment had begun. Both sides had drawn blood. Both were suffering from the blows. And it was about to get worse.

The candidate's opponent was a much older man who claimed to have religion on his side. He was a preacher, well known in his day, and eager to bring faith into the fight. The two had clashed some years before, and it had been an ugly, religious brawl. The preacher had won then and planned to now using the same tactics as before.

The candidate was unprepared. The press reported that he was an "infidel," that his wife was a coldhearted Episcopalian, and that he had been heard to say that church members were no better than drunkards. Rumors spread that the candidate did not accept Jesus Christ or the doctrines of the Christian faith. In fact, sources reported that the candidate had once claimed "Christ was a bastard."

At first the candidate only whimpered. The preacher, he complained, "never heard me utter a word in any way indicating my opinions on religious matters, in his life." Then he attacked his opponent personally, reminding the press that the preacher was unlikable, the kind of man who once attended a church service and afterward complained that a deacon's prayer was so cold that "three prayers like that would freeze hell over."

None of this quelled the storm, and the candidate realized he had to address the questions about his faith directly. It was true, he admitted publicly, that he was not a member of any Christian church. But it was a lie that he had ever spoken against the Scriptures or had expressed disrespect for religion in general. Yes, in his early life he had attacked the supernatural claims of Christianity, but that was then. Now, he could not conceive of supporting a man for office whom he knew to be an enemy of religion. His opponent already knew this, yet circulated lies about him for mere political gain.

The bludgeoning continued. The gashes deepened. Yet, at long last, the candidate won.[1]

He was, though, a wounded victor. The religious pummeling he had endured drew him no closer to God and left him with more doubts and confusion than he had before. How could he embrace the faith of his opponent—a preacher, no less—who dealt in lies and sliced open men's souls merely to win votes?

The passing years alone gave their answer, for with time and distance came healing. The candidate would continue in politics, rising eventually to high office. There would be tragedy: the deaths of sons, a bloody war, and the hardships of life and manhood common to the ages. While still in office, the candidate would find his God and a faith so strong that he offered it to his nation in some of the most tenderly wrenching terms of any statesman in history.

So deep was this change in his soul that on the night he died, he turned to his wife and said that when his service to his country was done, he wanted to go to Jerusalem and walk in the steps of his Master. It was not to be, but the hope—and the faith that fueled this hope—did much to heal his nation.

This infidel? This nonbeliever? This candidate who some said lacked enough faith to warrant public office?

His name was Abraham Lincoln.

ON HIS THIRD MEETING WITH PRESIDENT GEORGE W. Bush, Barack Obama found himself on the receiving end of political advice. "You've got a bright future," the president said. "Very bright. But I've been in this town awhile and, let me tell you, it can be tough. When you get a lot of attention like you've been getting, people start gunnin' for ya. And it won't necessarily just be coming from my side, you understand. From yours, too. Everybody'll be waiting for you to slip, know what I mean? So watch yourself."

While Obama was still wondering about the president's warning, Bush seemed to want to explain his sense of connection to the young senator from Illinois.

"You know, me and you got something in common," Bush offered.

"What's that?"

"We both had to debate Alan Keyes. That guy's a piece of work, isn't he?"[2]

It was a sentiment Obama could welcome with a laugh, for he had indeed debated Alan Keyes—and defeated him decisively in his Senate race of 2004. Yet the memory likely made him wince, for the battle between Obama and Keyes for the U.S. Senate became a contest of worldviews, a microcosm of the larger religious issues at play in American politics. The experience was painful, and thrust Obama into a season of soul-searching and intellectual reexamination that tempered the religious sword he would later wield on the national stage.

The battle with Keyes came about through a process that caused some to label Obama "the luckiest politician in the entire fifty states."[3] Upon announcing his candidacy for the Senate, Obama joined a crowded Democratic primary field. Almost immediately, his two strongest opponents sustained fatal political damage: one under charges of improperly bundling campaign contributions and another when details of his divorce showed allegations of spousal abuse. Obama won the primary and then faced Republican Jack Ryan in the general election. As David Mendell has observed in *Obama: From*

Promise to Power, Ryan "looked as if he had been ordered from central casting. He was tall, lean, square-jawed, Ivy League-educated and well spoken. After becoming rich in investment banking, he spent a few years teaching in a private high school in Chicago's inner city and articulated a Jack Kemp-esque, pro-business brand of compassionate conservatism."[4]

The looming campaign promised to offer a classic American political fight, made thrilling by the vast gap between the candidates in personality, principle, and money. Yet it was not to be. Weeks into the campaign, details of Ryan's divorce from actress Jeri Ryan became public. The tales of bizarre sexual rituals, of a wife forced into degrading public sex in clubs around the world, was too much for Ryan's "family values" image to sustain. Within weeks, he dropped out of the race, leaving his party in crisis.

Then came Alan Keyes, admittedly dragged into the fray from Maryland by a desperate Illinois GOP scrambling at the last minute to find a viable candidate. Long an articulate voice of conservative values—and with credentials from Harvard, the U.S. Foreign Service, the Reagan administration, and two presidential races—he had acquired a reputation as a speechmaker and debater of both laser precision and poetic sense reminiscent of the black pulpit. He entered the Illinois race largely to advance the conservative agenda. As he explained to a National Public Radio audience, "You are doing what you believe to be required by your respect for God's will, and I think that that's what I'm doing in Illinois."[5]

From the beginning, Keyes faced heated criticism for being

a "carpetbagger" because he had never lived in Illinois, he had harshly criticized Hillary Clinton of Arkansas for her Senate run in New York—"pure and planned selfish ambition" he called it—and his only property in the state was a rented apartment in downtown Chicago. He had clearly been recruited to counter Obama's star-crossed image. As one state senator crassly admitted to Obama, "We got our own Harvard-educated conservative black guy to go up against the Harvard-educated liberal black guy. He may not win, but at least he can knock that halo off your head."[6]

Obama found Keyes to be a cross between "Pentecostal preacher and William F. Buckley," a man who couldn't "conceal what he clearly considered to be his moral and intellectual superiority."[7] Keyes's soaring oratory and sharp criticism were unapologetically Christian, conservative, and moralistic. He insisted that Obama was encouraging a black genocide by supporting abortion. He alleged that the young state senator evidenced a "breathtaking naiveté" about the Iraq war, displayed "ignorance" of the U.S. Constitution, and endorsed a "hedonistic" gay agenda. Perhaps most injurious, Keyes accused Obama of being a man of faith only "when it's convenient to get votes. At the hard points when that faith must be followed and explained to folks and stood up for and witnessed to . . . he pleads separation of church and state, something found nowhere in the Constitution, and certainly found nowhere in the Scripture as such."[8]

In short, Keyes insisted, "Christ would not vote for Barack

Obama because Barack Obama has voted to behave in a way that it is inconceivable for Christ to have behaved."[9] As the *Chicago Tribune* recounted one dramatic moment during a debate, Keyes spread his arms apart and said, "Christ is over here, Senator Obama is over there: the two don't look the same."[10]

This onslaught rattled Obama at first, but he soon recovered. He countered that he didn't need Keyes to lecture him on Christianity: "That's why I have a pastor. That's why I have a Bible. That's why I have my own prayer. And I don't think any of you are particularly interested in having Mr. Keyes lecture you about your faith. What you're interested in is solving problems like jobs and health care and education. I'm not running to be the minister of Illinois. I'm running to be its United States senator."[11]

When Keyes charged that Liberalism is immoral, Obama fired back, "I think there's something immoral about somebody who's lost their job after 20 years, has no health care, or [is] seeing their pension threatened. I think there's something immoral about young people who've got the grades and the drive to go to college but just don't have the money. There are millions of people all across this state that are having a

> "What you're interested in is solving problems like jobs and health care and education. I'm not running to be the minister of Illinois. I'm running to be its United States senator."

THE FAITH OF BARACK OBAMA

tough time, and Washington is not listening to them, and neither is Mr. Keyes."[12]

It was a faith-based political fight on a grand scale, but Keyes never really had a chance. He was outmanned. He was outspent. He had entered the race far too late. When it was all over, Obama won with a margin of more than 40 percent of the vote. Exit polls showed that while many voters admired Keyes, they thought that his eccentricities—during one interview he inexplicably began singing a Negro spiritual and during another shocked even Republicans by suggesting tax breaks for all blacks with slave ancestry—made him unfit for office. As Obama later concluded, "Alan Keyes was an ideal opponent; all I had to do was keep my mouth shut and start planning my swearing-in ceremony."[13]

But this flippant dismissal belied the uncertainty that Keyes awakened in Obama's soul. He couldn't move on, couldn't bury Keyes in memory as he had in his landslide political victory. He was still wrestling even months later, as he had been during the campaign, still struggling with what had happened, with the fallout in his own mind from the clash of worldviews that he and Keyes represented.

It galled him that Keyes "claimed to speak for my religion, and my God. He claimed knowledge of certain truths. Mr. Obama says he's a Christian, he was saying, and yet he supports a lifestyle that the Bible calls an abomination. Mr. Obama says he's a Christian, but supports the destruction of innocent and sacred life."[14]

Reflecting on the campaign, Obama knew his answers were stale: "And so what would my supporters have me say? How should I respond? Should I say that a literalist reading of the Bible was folly? Should I say that Mr. Keyes, who is a Roman Catholic, should ignore the teachings of the Pope?" This was a man second-guessing himself, irritated that he had not seized the moment with grace: "Unwilling to go there, I answered with what has come to be the typically liberal response in such debates—namely, I said that we live in a pluralistic society, that I can't impose my own religious views on another, that I was running to be the U.S. Senator of Illinois and not the Minister of Illinois."[15]

But his rhetoric had fallen flat, and he knew it. Even more, he knew he had missed a grand opportunity. The debate between the two eloquent black men "reflected a broader debate we've been having in this country for the last thirty years over the role of religion in politics." This debate raged within Obama as well, and for many months he continued to ponder what had happened in the fall of 2004. By the summer of 2006, he seemed to have settled his mind and resolved his beliefs about faith and democracy. At a conference titled "From Poverty to Opportunity: A Covenant for a New America," sponsored by Jim Wallis's progressive Sojourners organization, Obama gave a speech which not only showed the fruits of his recent soul-searching but also served as a declaration of values for the rising Religious Left.[16]

Warning Progressives that "if we don't reach out to

evangelical Christians and other religious Americans and tell them what we stand for, then the Jerry Falwells and Pat Robertsons and Alan Keyeses will continue to hold sway," Obama reminded the political Left that in America "90 percent of us believe in God, 70 percent affiliate themselves with an organized religion, 38 percent call themselves committed Christians, and substantially more people in America believe in angels than they do in evolution."

> *"If we don't reach out to evangelical Christians and other religious Americans and tell them what we stand for, then the Jerry Falwells and Pat Robertsons and Alan Keyeses will continue to hold sway,"*

Then, in a surprising break from the secular legacy of the political Left, Obama charged that "secularists are wrong when they ask believers to leave their religion at the door before entering into the public square . . . to say that men and women should not inject their 'personal morality' into public policy debates is a practical absurdity. Our law is by definition a codification of morality, much of it grounded in the Judeo-Christian tradition."

Progressives, then, should shed their antireligion biases, perhaps finding "some overlapping values that both religious and secular people share when it comes to the moral and material direction of our country . . . And we might realize that we have the ability to reach out to the evangelical community and engage millions of religious Americans in the larger project of American renewal."

This, then, was Obama's message to the political Left: stop rejecting people of faith and instead find common ground. Yet, to the Right, he also offered "some truths they need to acknowledge." First, conservatives, particularly those of the Religious Right, need to recognize the "critical role that the separation of church and state has played" in America. "Whatever we once were," Obama insisted, "we are no longer just a Christian nation; we are also a Jewish nation, a Muslim nation, a Buddhist nation, a Hindu nation, and a nation of nonbelievers."

The paragraph that followed this admonition was one of the most revealing of his speech:

And even if we did have only Christians in our midst, if we expelled every non-Christian from the United States of America, whose Christianity would we teach in the schools? Would we go with James Dobson's, or Al Sharpton's? Which passages of Scripture should guide our public policy? Should we go with Leviticus, which suggests slavery is okay and that eating shellfish is abomination? How about Deuteronomy, which suggests stoning your child if he strays from the faith? Or should we just stick to the Sermon on the Mount—a passage that is so radical that it's doubtful that our own Defense Department would survive its application? So, before we get carried away, let's read our Bibles. Folks haven't been reading their Bibles.

While insisting on the necessity of the separation between church and state, Obama showed balance, calling for what some termed afterward "First Amendment sanity":

But a sense of proportion should also guide those who police the boundaries between church and state. Not every mention of God in public is a breach to the wall of separation—context matters. It is doubtful that children reciting the Pledge of Allegiance feel oppressed or brainwashed as a consequence of muttering the phrase "under God." I didn't. Having voluntary student prayer groups use school property to meet should not be a threat, any more than its use by the High School Republicans should threaten Democrats.

In light of American pluralism, then, Obama insisted that religion ought to change its voice when entering the public square. "Democracy demands," he argued:

that the religiously motivated translate their concerns into universal, rather than religion-specific, values. It requires that their proposals be subject to argument, and amenable to reason. I may be opposed to abortion for religious reasons, but if I seek to pass a law banning the practice, I cannot simply point to the teachings of my church or evoke God's will. I have to explain why abortion violates some principle that is accessible to people of all faiths, including those with no faith at all.

Finally, and with the taunts of Alan Keyes still vivid in his mind, Obama offered:

> I am hopeful that we can bridge the gaps that exist and over-
> come the prejudices each of us bring to this debate. And I have
> faith that millions of believing Americans want that to happen.
> No matter how religious they may or may not be, people are
> tired of seeing faith used as a tool of attack. They don't want
> faith used to belittle or to divide. They're tired of hearing folks
> deliver more screed than sermon. Because in the end, that's not
> how they think about faith in their own lives.

The speech would prove to be among the most significant of Obama's life. With its tone of moderation, its welcome of faith into the public square, and yet its insistence that people of faith conduct themselves in public debate according to democratic values, it became what Obama had intended: a call to reform, a redefinition of religion's role in American political life. Soon, his words were debated on cable news programs, heard by tens of thousands on YouTube, and argued fiercely on Web sites from every political perspective.

Columnist E. J. Dionne of the *Washington Post* declared that it was "the most important pronouncement by a Democrat on faith and politics since John F. Kennedy's Houston speech in 1960 declaring his independence from the Vatican."[17] Even some conservatives were impressed. Peter Wood of New York's King's College admitted in *National Review* that Obama's "attempt to graft the citrus branch of Christian piety to the hemlock tree of the Democratic Party just might bear fruit."[18]

Thoroughly unimpressed, though, was the secular Left. "More God and country crap from the party that ought to know better," steamed one blogger on a Left-leaning Web site. Believing that religion has no legitimate role in government or public policy, those who embraced a more traditional, secular liberalism could find in Obama's speech little more than betrayal, merely the religious dance now required of politicians in the wake of the Religious Right.

And yet it was from this very Religious Right that the most heated criticism of Obama's speech arose. Though he had tried to address this segment of America—though he had tried to call them to the public square while urging reason and a more democratic tone—Obama's speech only exposed the vast differences between the Religious Right and a newly emerging Religious Left. Understanding these differences, indeed, confronting the fiery opposition of the right in its most full-throated form, is essential to understanding not only some of the battle lines in current American politics but also the religious opposition Obama is likely to face throughout his public career. It is the Religious Right—and its insistence on a political worldview that arises unchecked from Scripture and contends unaltered in the public square—which is Obama's primary intellectual opposition. That Right has been the keeper of the religious flame in American politics; the primary guardian of a biblically based form of public policy; and the most vocal critic of civil religion, the faith they accuse Obama of fashioning from the secular values of the American way. And that Religious Right suspects the sincerity of Obama's speech, particularly when they consider his response to what is for them the watershed issue of this generation: abortion.

FOR MOST RELIGIOUS CONSERVATIVES, OBAMA'S SPEECH was merely Liberalism repackaged for a new, more faith-sensitive generation. America is no longer a Christian nation, and traditionalists should wake up to the realities of a pluralistic society, they heard Obama saying. No longer are the commands of God welcomed in the public square. Now people of faith must express themselves in something other than "religion-specific values." And that call to "the larger project of American renewal"? That was just Obama's vision for big-government intrusion, a code phrase for the New Frontier and Great Society programs of a new age.

It was true, some admitted, that there had been concessions in the speech to the concerns of traditional Christians. Obama had, after all, rebuked the Left

> Obama had rebuked the Left for forcing people of faith to leave their beliefs outside of the public square. He had also conceded that not every public expression of faith violates the separation of church and state.

for forcing people of faith to leave their beliefs outside of the public square. He had also conceded that not every public expression of faith violates the separation of church and state. Still, it was not enough, for sounding loud from every page of the speech—as religious conservatives heard it—was an apparent call for traditional Christians to surrender their values, to become "politically correct," in order to be taken seriously by nonbelievers in the nation's public debates. This is what some referred to with sarcasm as Obama's call to join the "American Church of Pluralism." They meant a temple of state religion in which all faiths are welcome but in which all must bow the knee to an official cult of reason, in which all have a claim, but only if they defer to the religious neutrality of the democratic way.

This charge is critical to understanding how the Religious Right perceives Obama's worldview. Like fiscal conservatives, religious conservatives have long resisted the bloated modern state, yet they have done so for more theological reasons. Religious conservatives warn that the overreaching, intrusive state will not simply silence traditional religions; it will become a religion of its own. This is the tendency of all tyrannical governments, they claim, from ancient Babylon and Rome to Nazi Germany and Stalinist Russia. No one recognized and celebrated this more than the German philosopher Friedrich Hegel, whom conservative scholars from Francis Schaeffer to Michael Novak quote in warning. "The State is the Divine Idea as it exists on earth," Hegel wrote. "We must therefore worship the

State as the manifestation of the Divine . . . The State is the march of God through the world."[19]

This view is exactly what alarms religious conservatives. The state as God. American values woven into a religion of its own. Traditional faith kneeling at the altar of the state. The idolatry of an American Shinto. And this is also what they fear in Obama when he declares to a reporter, "Alongside my own deep personal faith, I am a follower, as well, of our civic religion."[20]

Conservatives suspect that this "civic religion" is Obama's ploy: a mask he uses to hide his political and theological liberalism. While sounding the symbolic language of the American experience—"the democratic way," the "neutral public square," "the equality of all religions"—he advances the cause of his oldline, statist liberalism. This civil religion, conservatives would say, is the culturally acceptable language in which he couches his ideals but conceals his agenda. And this is all the more offensive to them because they believe that the very civil religion that Obama would use to replace traditional religion is without any power for solving societal ills. It is, in Will Herberg's oftquoted phrase, "a religiousness without religion, a religiousness with almost any kind of content or none, a way of sociability or 'belonging' rather than a way of reorienting life to God."[21]

> This civil religion, conservatives would say, is the culturally acceptable language in which he couches his ideals but conceals his agenda.

Thus, what Obama's civil religion actually does, some allege, is give people a watered-down religion of Americanism but insulate them from the raw but healing truth of revealed religion. In other words, it replaces traditional religion with a bland political religiosity that creates a mood without offering power. It is merely faith in faith rather than faith in God. As Herbert Schlossberg wrote in *Idols for Destruction*:

> A religious statement, on the other hand, which says "do not be conformed to the values of society" swings an axe at the trunk of civil religion. Civil religion eases tensions, where biblical religion creates them. Civil religion papers over the cracks of evil, and biblical religion strips away the covering, exposing the nasty places. Civil religion prescribes aspirin for cancer, and biblical religion insists on the knife.[22]

For the Religious Right, then, civil religion is not unlike Roman emperor Alexander Severus adding an image of Christ to the gods he worshipped in his private chapel. Indeed, civil religion is exactly like President Eisenhower insisting that American government makes no sense "unless it is founded in a deeply felt religious faith—and I don't care what it is."[23] And it is also like Barack Obama using social justice concerns as a call to religious neutrality in honor of the secular American way.

For many evangelicals, Roman Catholics, and religious conservatives, then, civil religion is a kind of idolatry. But they are not surprised to find it coming from Barack Obama. Civil religion, they would argue, is the natural product of Obama's theological liberalism, for when religion is drained of its traditional meaning, it admits to any meaning. That Obama applies the meaning of Scripture to the work of the state, that he calls for a high wall of separation between church and state, and that he insists on the use of nonreligious language in the public square, is exactly what religious conservatives expect. These are tactics to silence the voice of faith, to destroy all gods that compete with the divine state, to demand the surrender of all values inconsistent with the official morality.

Nowhere do religious conservatives find Obama more a shining symbol of this civil religion than in the matter of abortion. This is, in their eyes, the issue that overshadows everything else in American public policy, and largely because abortion as they understand it involves the death of human beings. Initially, they thought Obama might be with them in their views. In his symposium speech, he had said, "I may be opposed to abortion for religious reasons, but if I seek to pass a law banning the practice, I cannot simply point to the teachings of my church or evoke God's will. I have to explain why abortion violates some principle that is accessible to people of all faiths, including those with no

> Nowhere do religious conservatives find Obama more a shining symbol of this civil religion than in the matter of abortion.

faith at all." Some conservatives began to suspect that he might actually believe privately that abortion is the taking of a human life. As he told *Christianity Today*, "I don't know anybody who is pro-abortion."[24]

Yet if he was sensitive to the ambivalence many Americans feel about abortion and the plight of the unborn, his voting record did not show it. As columnist Amanda Carpenter complained in the staunchly conservative *Human Events* some months after Obama's speech, "Senator Barack Obama portrays himself as a thoughtful Democrat who carefully considers both sides of controversial issues, but his radical stance on abortion puts him further left on that issue than even NARAL Pro-Choice America."[25]

Carpenter went on to explain that in 2002, Obama had voted in the Illinois senate against the Induced Infant Liability Act, which would have protected babies who survived late-term abortions. The act sought the same treatment for babies who survived abortions as was routinely provided for babies born premature and thus given lifesaving medical attention. The same year that the Illinois legislature debated the act, a similar federal bill—called the Born-Alive Infants Protection Act—became law with only fifteen members of the U.S. House opposing it. Indeed, the National Abortion Rights Action League (NARAL), one of the nation's most powerful pro-abortion advocacy organizations, even issued a statement declaring that "NARAL does not oppose passage of the Born Alive Infants Protection Act [because] floor debate served to clarify the bill's intent and assure us that it is not targeted at *Roe v. Wade* or a woman's right to choose."[26] Despite even NARAL having no objection to such bills, Obama voted against the Illinois version in the senate.

Jill Stanek, a registered delivery-ward nurse who became an advocate for the bill after seeing babies born alive and then left to die, testified twice before Obama in support of the bill, as she had earlier before Congress. "I brought pictures in and presented them to the committee . . . trying to show them unwanted babies were being cast aside. Babies the same age were being treated if they were wanted! And those pictures didn't faze [Obama] at all," she remembered.[27]

Transcripts of the hearings reveal that at the end of testimony, Obama thanked Stanek for being "very clear and forthright," but he expressed his concern at Stanek suggesting that "doctors really don't care about children who are being born with a reasonable prospect of life because they are so locked into their pro-abortion views that they would watch an infant that is viable die." Obama concluded, "That may be your assessment, and I don't see any evidence of that. What we are doing here is to create one more burden on a woman and I can't support that."[28]

Obama later explained that he voted against the bill because the language was so broad that it would have disallowed all abortions. Still, the staunchly pro-life Religious Right couldn't understand a man who claimed to be a Christian but voted more pro-choice than even NARAL required. Moreover, as he later admitted, he wasn't sure how his pro-choice politics squared with his faith. "I cannot claim infallibility in my support of abortion rights," he wrote in *The Audacity of Hope*.

I must admit that I may have been infected with society's pre-dilections and attributed them to God; that Jesus' call to love one another might demand a different conclusion; and that in years hence I may be seen as someone who was on the wrong side of history. I don't believe such doubts make me a bad Christian. I believe they make me human, limited in my understandings of God's purpose and therefore prone to sin.[29]

While Obama remained uncertain about abortion, he nevertheless voted for babies who survived abortion to then be exposed and left to die. This he did, many of his frustrated critics believed, kneeling before the altar of a "choice at all costs" political correctness—under cover of the civil religion that he admits to laying alongside his Christian faith.

This willingness to surrender faith to politics, as so many of his fellow Christians saw it, brought into question Obama's attempts to heal the nation's religious divide. It defined the distinction in the eyes of the Right between Keyes and Obama, between Jerusalem and Athens, between the bold political vision of Christian founding fathers and the weak, statist theology of a modern civil faith.

Nevertheless, the speech—soon titled the "Call to Renewal" speech—became Barack Obama's religious declaration of intent. If he had summoned the Religious Left in his Democratic National Convention speech of 2004, he gave the movement a blueprint for cultural impact in 2006.

The speech, and the hard-won clarity that produced it, came

just in time. Barely six months later, he announced that he was a candidate for the presidency. What followed would prove to be one of the most religiously charged political contests in American history. Yet in the debates, in the "faith forums," in the controversies that arose from the teachings of his church, and in the taunts from both the Right and the Left, Barack Obama knew who he was religiously,

If he had summoned the Religious Left in his Democratic National Convention speech of 2004, he gave the movement a blueprint for cultural impact in 2006.

knew what he believed about religion and the state. No more the "typical liberal responses." No more a retreat behind the separation of church and state. Now his worldview was integrated and firm. He was a liberal Christian, embracing a faith-based liberal political vision, and he planned to take both into his nation's corridors of power.

5

A New Band of Brothers

It had not always been easy for Pastor Joel Hunter to be Barack Obama's friend. Suspicion of their relationship had arisen from both sides of the political aisle and more than a few had accused Hunter of abandoning his principles for visibility and fame. He was a "turncoat," had "gone liberal," had forgotten what God had called him to do. It had all been enmeshed in the blood sport that was now American politics and for Hunter there had been the torturous seasons, the agony of taking verbal hits for his friend while having his motives and character maligned.

But on this day—on this dark and tearful day—Joel Hunter learned, if he had never known before, what kind of friend Barack Obama could be.

His relationship with the young politician had started with a handwritten note that came after the candidate's "A More

Perfect Union" speech in 2008. While the nation was astir with the racial themes Obama had explored—within a week nearly two million Americans had viewed the speech on YouTube alone—Hunter offered some comments for an article in the *New York Times*. He was an odd choice for this. He was the pastor of a twelve-thousand-member, nearly all-white church in central Florida called Northland and was certainly no expert on racial affairs. Still, he had been stirred by Obama's speech and as a prominent pastor wanted to help heal the racial wounds the nation endured. The speech was a "Rorschach inkblot test" for the country, he told the *New York Times*. "It calls out of you what is already in you," he insisted, meaning that if a person was indifferent to race the speech would mean little, but those who cared could not help but be incited to act. He told the *Times* what he and his staff had concluded at their regular Wednesday morning meeting: "We want for there to be healing and reconciliation, but unless it's raised in a very public manner, it's tough for us in our regular conversation to raise it."[1] When Barack Obama read these comments in the March 20 edition of the paper, he decided to write Pastor Hunter a note. "I'd like to catch up with you someday," he said.

So it began. Before long Joshua DuBois, the Obama campaign's director of faith-based outreach, made contact with Hunter and the two men became friends. Then there was that first phone conversation with Obama and a connection that strengthened in conversation and prayer. Hillary Clinton contacted Hunter, as did Mike Huckabee, and Hunter was gracious with each, but he resonated most with the young senator from Illinois and his eagerness to bring meaningful change to America. Then came the invitation to give the benediction at the Democratic National Convention in Denver that August.

The opportunity had given him pause, for Joel Hunter was no politically ambiguous evangelical pastor. He was a man clear about his principles. He objected to abortion and gay marriage, even spoke openly about being a part of the "constructive Religious Right." In fact, in 2006 he had gone so far as to accept the presidency of the Christian Coalition, the conservative advocacy group founded by religious broadcaster Pat Robertson. Before he could take office, though, things had changed. The board of the Christian Coalition voted not to expand its agenda to matters like poverty and the environment under Hunter's leadership, matters that were clearly Christian concerns. They obviously did not want to alienate the Republican base, did not want to allow much distance from the Republican Party platform. In addition, Hunter was saddened to see that the Republican leadership, in turn, was taking its cues from

> *Hunter was saddened to see that the Republican leadership was taking its cues from Rush Limbaugh and that niche groups and cable television scream-fests politicized even the Christian believers that he had hoped to lead.*

Rush Limbaugh and that niche groups and cable television scream-fests politicized even the Christian believers that he had hoped to lead. In frustration and disillusionment, he walked away from the presidency of the Coalition and decided to speak the political implications of Scripture to whoever was willing to hear. When he later befriended Joshua DuBois, when he met Barack Obama, and when the chance to pray at the Democratic Convention came his way, he knew that, despite his political differences, he should be faithful to the role his God was calling him to play.

So he prayed at the Democratic convention and later prayed with Obama privately before one of the presidential debates. When Obama ascended to the Oval Office and Joshua DuBois asked Hunter to be on a team of spiritual advisors who would pray with the president and help keep him strong, the pastor agreed. This angered some of his friends on the right. A few parishioners even left his church in disgust, but Hunter believed that he was fulfilling the work of a pastor, speaking the truth to both sides of the political aisle just as Jesus would want him to do. And so he prayed regularly with the president and wrote devotionals to help feed him from the Scriptures and endured the opposition from those who felt betrayed.

Then came that horrible, agonizing day. Among the delights of Joel Hunter's life was his granddaughter, Ava. She was sweet and bubbly with sparkling eyes and dimpled cheeks sure to melt a grandfather's heart. He called her his "little warrior." In June 2010, when she was only five, Ava was diagnosed with a rare form of brain tumor—glioblastoma multiforme. It is the most aggressive possible kind of brain tumor—the type that led to the death of Ted Kennedy—but it is rare in children. When news of Ava's condition spread, the National Institute of Health contacted Hunter and said they simply didn't have any protocols for such a thing. "Among five year olds, you can count the occurrences on one hand," he was told. And the pastor began to realize that his beloved granddaughter might die.

The next day, Hunter's phone rang. It was the White House operator.

"Dr. Hunter, will you stand by for a call from the president."

"Yes."

And then, in a moment, "Joel, this is Barack. I just heard about Ava. I just had to call and tell you that Michelle and I are praying for you. If there is anything we can do we want to do it."

Unable to meet Obama's informality, Hunter replied, "Thank you, Mr. President. That's very kind. We have checked and there is no traditional treatment which has proven effective. We're at a loss. But I appre . . ."

"No. Stop that." Obama interrupted impatiently. And then, gently, "I really mean it, Joel. Anything I can do I want to do."

Hunter could take no more, and began to weep.

Then began the reversal. The man who had pastored the president now sat silently in tears as the president became, for a few moments, the pastor Hunter desperately needed. "Joel, I want you to remember that God has got you here. He's not going to let you go. He will walk all the way through this with you. You remember this. God isn't going to let go of you. We've got to hold on to our faith in God." And so it went. While Hunter wept, the president of the United States helped his friend find strength in God. It continued for many minutes and then, finally, Obama said, "Please tell your family that Michelle and I are praying for them and our heart goes out to them."

"Thank you, sir," Hunter said, and the two hung up. It struck Hunter that Obama had been the first to call.

What followed were some of the worst weeks of Joel Hunter's life. His granddaughter was forced to undergo a grueling surgery to remove the tumor. There was hope for a season and then, within seven weeks, the tumor grew back even bigger than before. On September 4, Ava died. Hunter was undone.

That same day the phone rang. "Dr. Hunter, will you stand by for a call from the president."

The pastor was surprised. He had just walked by the television and had seen Obama giving a speech in Minnesota. Hunter was sure the president could not know already about Ava.

"Yes, I will stand by," Hunter told the operator.

Soon, the president came on the line, obviously broken-hearted. "Joel, this is Barack. I've just heard. I'm so sorry. You will be in my prayers. Michelle and I are with you. We are trusting God to go through this with you."

"You are so kind, Mr. President. Thank you. This means a great deal to me."

Then, as before—as Hunter's words failed him—the president began to minister. Again, the encouragement. Again, the bits of scripture and assurances of God's grace. Again, the faith of a president offered to his friend.

Soon, Hunter began to realize how long they had been on the phone. He could picture in his mind's eye aides tapping their watches and Secret Service agents looking nervously about. He had been with the president during those moments and did not wish now to be rude. But Obama seemed to have nowhere else to be. He was focused on his friend. Gently, Hunter began to move the president of the United States off the phone. It was not an easy thing to do.

Finally, "Your concern touches me, Mr. President. Thank you for calling."

"We are praying for you, Joel," Obama said before hanging up. "I am with you in this. You are not alone."[2]

THE BARACK OBAMA OF THE STORY TOLD ABOVE IS NOT one most Americans would know. His critics—those who suspect him religiously or who think he is a closet Muslim—would be stunned to find the president "pastoring" anyone in the name of Christ. The vast majority of Americans who are simply confused by Obama's faith would be surprised to find him drawing so deeply from the words of the Bible and the Christian tradition. Even supporters who believe he is a Christian might well be astonished to hear the Columbia and Harvard scholar, trained in the art of emotional detachment by his humanist mother, pouring out his faith so fully, so passionately. Yet what each of these

> *His critics—those who suspect him religiously or who think he is a closet Muslim—would be stunned to find the president "pastoring" anyone in the name of Christ.*

portions of American society do not know, cannot have seen, is the spiritual transformation that Barack Obama has undergone since becoming president.

We must remember that when Obama entered the Oval Office he was armed only with the religious training he had received during twenty years under the ministry of Jeremiah Wright. And yet, just months before his election, he had found portions of that training wanting—had tested the spirit of his pastor, distanced himself, and set off in a different direction. As the Obamas moved into the White House, this new direction was undefined, uncharted—fueled more by a certainty of what Barack Obama did not want to be rather than what he felt called to become.

It was just at this time that Obama began to be influenced by men of a different spirit, of a different theological and spiritual stream, than what he had previously known. They were more a band of brothers than the single spiritual father Jeremiah Wright had been, more a team around him than a mentor above. They have urged the president toward a deeper relationship with God. They have worked to root him in the meaning of Scripture. They have supported him through intense prayer and the encouragement of a dynamic Christian faith. It has changed him. As Joel Hunter has said,

> Trinity United Church of Christ gave Barack Obama two things: the born again experience and a social vision. But he did not gain much theological training through those years. He has now, during his first years in office, been exposed to more spiritual depth and biblical theology than he had in all his prior years.[3]

This has led to a quiet spiritual transformation in the life of Barack Obama. It has been kept private, intentionally hidden from public view, largely to preserve it and keep it a matter of heart. But it is this new spiritual depth in the life of the president that has allowed him to pastor a famous pastor during the worst crisis of the man's life. It is also this newfound well of inspiration that may serve to shape the soul of Barack Obama for the rest of his days.

THE MOST INFLUENTIAL OF THIS NEW BAND OF BROTHERS is Joshua DuBois, best known as the young head of the Office of Faith-Based and Neighborhood Partnerships. But DuBois is something more. *Time* magazine has called him "Obama's Pastor-in-Chief" and this is because the gifted African American Pentecostal has done more than perhaps any other person to assure a vital spirituality in the life of Barack Obama and to shape the religious vision of the Obama presidency.[4]

DuBois was born in Bar Harbor, Maine, but then spent his youth in Nashville, Tennessee, and Xenia, Ohio, defined largely by the work of his stepfather, a minister in the African Methodist Episcopal Church.

> "I had a pastor's kid distance from Christ largely because of all the religious busyness," he recalls. "My family sat at the forefront of the church but I was cynical about the whole thing. By the time I neared college, I rejected all things spiritual and had no intention of continuing to go to church.[5]

If his faith left him disillusioned, his vision for social change did not. Activism was in his blood. His grandmother had taken part in the Nashville sit-ins of the 1960s. Taking up her gauntlet, DuBois announced himself as a force for change when he was a seventeen-year-old freshman at Boston University. He had become enraged when New York policemen fired forty-one bullets into an unarmed Guinean immigrant name Amadou Diallo. The case received international attention, but DuBois lodged a protest in his own unique way. He decided to stand in front of the Martin Luther King Jr. memorial in Boston holding a sign that read, "NO MORE." He remained in place for forty-one hours, one for every bullet that entered the body of the unarmed Diallo.

As certain as he was about his social causes he was still uncertain spiritually. In time, a friend named Eugene Schneburg invited him to attend a tiny church of twenty-five members that met in a nearby school auditorium. It was grandly called Calvary Praise and Worship Center. There was no choir, no liturgy, but DuBois had never experienced anything like it. The speaker that day was Warren Collins and he delivered

> the most personal message about Christ I had ever heard, about how he wanted a relationship with me and not an institution, not the formality I had known. I felt like the Holy Spirit spoke to me. I can't say there weren't glimmers of a Christian walk before then. My parents did wonderful things and I knew it. But that was the day I came back to my faith.[6]

This was in the fall of 2000. Before long, DuBois would experience the baptism of the Holy Spirit, the greater filling of the soul by the spirit of God that defines Pentecostals.

He would graduate from Boston University in 2003 and go on to earn a master's degree from Princeton's Woodrow Wilson School of Public and International Affairs. He then set himself toward law school at Georgetown University. No sooner had he begun, though, when the senatorial campaign of a young politician from Illinois captured his imagination. What unfolded soon after is a tale still told with laughter by White House staff. DuBois was so eager to help Obama's cause that he decided to leave law school to work on the candidate's campaign. The now ex-law student sent an application to campaign headquarters. Not long after, a form letter arrived—rejecting him. Determined, DuBois drove to Obama's offices, besieged staffers, and finally won an interview. Wisely, he was hired to work in the arena of faith-based outreach.

He proved a brilliant strategist and networker, a conscientious political operative whose sincere faith inspired both loyalty and support for Obama. By the time the young senator announced his candidacy for president, DuBois had become such a valuable asset that he was named national director of religious affairs and put in charge of a team of eight staffers and hundreds of volunteers. He was still in his twenties, but he left a defining mark on one of the most remarkable political ascents in history. It was DuBois who designed the Obama campaign's efforts to win evangelicals, like the outreach to young voters called "The Joshua Generation," language taken from the youth ministries of evangelical churches nationwide. It was DuBois who assembled twenty-five leading religious conservatives in Chicago during the summer of 2008 so they could grill Obama about what he believed. And it was DuBois who engineered Obama's appearance at Rick Warren's Presidential Forum during the height of the campaign and then worked to have Warren invited to pray at Obama's inauguration despite the famous pastor's deep policy differences with the president-elect.

Just as significant, throughout the campaign DuBois urged Obama to connect with supportive pastors, facilitated prayer times before debates or critical speeches, and generally tried to make sure that his candidate had some meaningful spiritual input. There was that phone call with T. D. Jakes in an L.A. hotel room and that other moment of heartfelt prayer with Dr. Joel

Hunter in the Green Room before a debate. Conference calls with as many as half a dozen pastors for prayer and encouragement were not unknown. DuBois engineered them all. Perhaps he sensed that Obama was religiously at sea. Perhaps he could feel the hurt in the Obama family at losing their church and connections of faith that had sustained them for decades. Perhaps he knew that the fuel of the young politician's fire was as much spiritual as it was intellectual and political and he felt it his duty to tend the flames well. Whatever the case, if DuBois was not Obama's new pastor, he was certainly Obama's personal spiritual facilitator.

Obama began to rely on him. On the night of the 2008 election, for example, when Obama sensed the presidency was about to be his but was still grieving the death of his grandmother only days before, DuBois pulled together T. D. Jakes, Pastor Joel Hunter, Kirbyjon Caldwell—a pastor to the Bush family—and Reverend Otis T. Moss to pray. They had done this before, on Obama's birthday and when DuBois saw that the need was great. That night's prayer was a "powerful time" and Obama felt it, he knew that the presence of such men of God in his life was important to the kind of man and president he wanted to be.

As the new administration dawned, DuBois received permission to create a group of "spiritual advisors," a team of pastors and religious leaders who would continue to tend the spiritual life of the new president. These included some of those who had prayed with or counseled Obama during the campaign as well as a broader group of African American pastors. DuBois coordinated these relationships to make sure that the president was receiving what he needed when he needed it and that all was kept from the public and the press.

Conference calls were the primary method of this ministry. At a time of DuBois's choosing, the spiritual advisors would be advised of a scheduled conference call for prayer, usually late in the afternoon of the president's busy day. Each would be given a number to call and a second code number for access. At the set time, after all the advisors had dialed in, the president would come on the line. There would be prayer. Then some would ask about the president's spiritual life, about how he was handling the hurtful blows of politics or if he was taking time for Scripture. There would be more prayer and words of encouragement to strengthen the president's soul. Never would these conversations stray into politics or matters of policy. They were designed simply to help Obama "get closer to God," to make his Christian faith relevant to the personal challenges he faced.

Upon occasion, some of these advisors had personal time with the president. T. D. Jakes has had such meetings, marked by intense prayer and great peals of laughter as the two men conversed. When Joel Hunter had similar meetings, he has found the president ready to "go deep," to allow the conversation to probe his heart and spiritual state. This openness, this transparency, is what has allowed Obama's spiritual advisors to have such a profound impact upon his life. These phone calls and meetings are not political theater, nor are they scripted and advertised to appease a religious base. Instead, they are just what they appear to be—professional religious leaders, charged with the care of the president's soul, doing their sacred work behind closed doors.

> *This openness, this transparency, is what has allowed Obama's spiritual advisors to have such a profound impact upon his life.*

To augment this ministry, DuBois has devised a unique devotional delivery system that makes use of the president's BlackBerry. Eager for Obama to have something in addition to the Bible that challenges him and helps him grow, DuBois sends a devotional by e-mail to the president's BlackBerry every day. Sometimes the words are taken from a Christian classic. He has used Oswald Chambers's *My Utmost for His Highest*, perhaps the best-known Christian devotional in the world, and he has also distilled selections from the writings of Dr. Howard Thurmond, the first black dean at Boston University's Marsh Chapel, whose writings inspired Martin Luther King Jr. Then DuBois has enlisted Obama's spiritual advisors themselves. Several of these, including Hunter, have been asked to write three-hundred-word daily devotionals that have been dubbed the "Reading the Red Series," because they are centered around the words of Jesus which appear in red ink in some Bibles. The selections include a scripture, a brief commentary, and a prayer. They are usually very personal and very pointed, as two examples from Hunter's pen reveal.

*Now after this the Lord appointed seventy others,
and sent them two and two ahead of Him to every
city and place where He Himself was going to
come . . . "Go your ways; behold, I send you out
as lambs in the midst of wolves."*

LUKE 10:1, 3 NASB

What kind of Shepherd sends his sheep out in the midst of wolves? One who has more confidence in His sheep than He has fear of the wolves.

My observation in forty years of being a pastor has been that God is not overly protective of His followers. Oh, there have been occasional miracles and rescues, things that have happened in response to prayer (or even without it) that have no earthly explanation. But for the most part, Christians have to go through what everyone else goes through.

God is more interested in us being emissaries and servants than He is guarding a protected class of special believers. He is more interested in being with us through the problems and the threats than He is in saving us from them. That is because He is more interested in building our character than He is in fixing our messes.

Some of the most loving decisions Becky and I made in raising our kids were to seldom rescue them, but to be available to them while they figured it out.

They became more confident and merciful because they walked through the difficulties instead of being able to avoid them.

Prayer: LORD, I do not desire rescue more than I desire Your closeness in the midst of problems.

And he took him to Jerusalem, and set him on the pinnacle of the temple, and said to him, "If you are the Son of God, throw yourself down from here; for it is written, 'He will give his angels charge of you, to guard you,' and 'On their hands they will bear you up, lest you strike your foot against a stone.'" And Jesus answered him, "It is written, 'You shall not tempt the Lord your God.'"

LUKE 4:9 ESV

The third temptation is to use religion in a spectacular way to expand one's own following. That the devil wanted Jesus to jump from the temple instead of pray inside it is no surprise. It is instructive to notice, however, the devices the devil uses to solicit.

In his crafty way, he incites doubt and pride at the same time, "If you are the Son of God . . ." Satan has a way of using the good to harm instead of help. One can almost hear the reiterations in everyday temptations. The teenage boy trying to seduce, "If you really loved me . . ." The leader tempted to bully, "If I am really the boss . . ." Temptation plays upon any existing insecurities to overplay any existing strengths.

The devil also quotes scripture to justify self-elevation and self-protection. Epidemic throughout the world now is the "prosperity gospel." It is the perversion of Christianity that persuades the worshipper that he / she should be exempted from the pain and struggle of life.

Jesus would have none of it. He was here to worship God and serve people, and the devil could go to hell.

Prayer: LORD, let me recognize temptation as a test You are giving me to improve me in Your service, and conform me to the image of Christ.

These times of prayer, personal challenge, counsel and reading have meant something new in Obama's life. As Hunter explains,

He was pretty busy during his Trinity years and so he wasn't learning very much. He had no significant theological training. He's now had more theological training in the last couple of years than in all his earlier life. Now he has answers he did not have then. The more we read Scripture, the more we understand Scripture and the more we understand truth. Obama is having a new encounter with truth.

Asked if Obama's earlier religious views have changed—about Scripture or the afterlife, for example—Hunter contends, "His views were not dogmatic when he issued them but they were where he was at the time. He is very much in transition. He would not hold most of those views now."[7]

The views that remain, though, are the core values that undergird his politics. From the beginning, Hunter discovered in Obama an eagerness to help the poor.

His focus was on the poor from the very first. He was focused on how the faith community could walk out its citizenship. When he approaches policy, he will always have a tender spot or an arch toward the vulnerable. He sees this as part of his faith. It is important to recall that he came to faith in the context of a community organizer, found a friend in Jesus in serving the poor. Christ had a special place in his heart for the poor and needy. The president always shows a predisposition toward those who cannot help themselves—a respect, a value for basic human dignity, for those who are marginalized.[8]

These, though, are the principles Americans expect of Obama. What the skeptical want to know, what the confused majority of Americans need answered, is whether Barack Obama is a serious,

> "There is simply no question about it," says Hunter, an unflinching evangelical. "Barack Obama is a born again man who has trusted in Jesus Christ with his whole heart."

committed Christian. Both DuBois and Hunter have had time to drill down into the deepest meaning of the president's spiritual life. Both conclude that Obama is truly, deeply "born again." "There is simply no question about it," says Hunter, an unflinching evangelical. "Barack Obama is a born again man who has trusted in Jesus Christ with his whole heart."[9] "Yes," says DuBois, "I know he's born again. I've asked him and he's described his faith in detail. He believes what the majority of Christians believe. And the experience of the presidency is strengthening his Christian muscles, making him a calm, confident, certain believer in Jesus Christ."[10]

IF JOSHUA DUBOIS CAN BE CREDITED WITH ASSEMBLING the band of brothers who have transformed Obama's religious life, both he and they have been helped in this cause by the man who has become, however unintentionally, the president's new pastor. His name is Carey Cash and though the White House understandably wishes to avoid any comparisons to Jeremiah Wright, it is important to know the character and spiritual passions of this engaging Navy chaplain whose duty it is to preach to the Obama family in the tiny Evergreen Chapel of Camp David, some seventy miles from the distracting stir of Washington DC.

To understand what Chaplain Cash might mean to the Obamas, we must first recognize the pain and disorientation they must have felt in the wake of the Jeremiah Wright episode. Obama has said,

> Let's be blunt, we were pretty affected by what happened at Trinity and the controversy surrounding Reverend Wright. That was deeply disturbing to us, and it was disappointing for us personally. It made us very sensitive to the fact that as president, the church we attend can end up being interpreted as speaking for us at all times.[11]

Adding to this turmoil was the chaos that ensued whenever the Obamas went in search of a new church in Washington DC. They visited several prominent African American congregations, including the city's famed Nineteenth Street Baptist Church. In each case, the story was the same. The joyous uproar of African American religious celebration allowed parishioners to sneak pictures or ask for autographs. Worship was nearly impossible. There could be no holy moment. An alternative was the staid formality of St. John's Episcopal Church—the traditional "Church of the Presidents" just across Lafayette Park from the White House. Here, at least, the ordered style would prevent the usual chaos. But it was a style foreign to Obama's soul and so he could find no rest there. In time, Barack and Michelle decided to simply make the little chapel at Camp David their religious home. Whatever the style of worship was, whoever was preaching the sermons, it was small, it was no chore to attend, and it was closed to the press and the public.

This decision brought Carey Cash into their lives, for not long before he had been named Camp David's chaplain. He was easy to like. He had a football lineman's body, a broad smile and piercing eyes. His manner was a blend of deep humility and manly confidence animated by an athlete's rowdiness and a warrior's zeal. It was intriguing, too, that he was country music star Johnny Cash's great-nephew and the brother of a former Miss America. Obama had simply never been close to anyone like this man before.

The two men could hardly have been from different backgrounds. While Obama had lived a fatherless, largely secular existence in exotic places like Hawaii and Indonesia, Cash had lived nearly the idyllic American life. He was born in Memphis, Tennessee, to the deeply religious family of a Navy fighter pilot. He first gained prominence on the high school football field before becoming an NCAA All-American offensive tackle at The Citadel. A career in the NFL loomed, but then came the crisis of his life: blurred vision and headaches lead to a dreaded diagnosis—an inoperable brain tumor. Football could no longer be his calling. "My life may have been as good as over in the eyes of some people," Cash later wrote, "but something deep inside was calling me to turn my eyes away from the situation and to trust God, who knew exactly what He was doing."[12]

He decided to attend Southwestern Baptist Theological Seminary at the urging of his Navy chaplain father-in-law. There followed a stint as a youth minister, some years as the pastor of a small church in Tennessee, and, gratefully, acceptance in the Naval Reserves when doctors certified Cash's tumor would not grow. One month before the horrors of September 11, 2001, he entered active-duty service and was assigned to the first Battalion, 5th Marine Regiment. In 2003, he found himself part of the first ground forces to enter Iraq.

He has recounted his experiences there in a book entitled, *A Table in the Presence: The Dramatic Account of How a U.S. Marine Battalion Experienced God's Presence Amidst the Chaos of the War in Iraq*. It is a thrilling tale. The chaplain prayed with Marines in sandy tents and sweaty amphibious assault vehicles, baptized men with canteen water and, on one occasion, completed a worship service under the spray of machine-gun fire. He also learned what it means to trust God under daily threat of death and to survive a firefight behind a "wall of angels." He would see men die and he would see them crack under the strain, but he would also emerge certain of miracles, certain of the calling of his God, and certain of the truth of the gospel.

It is this spiritual passion and yet engaging brand of earthiness, this familiarity with suffering and yet faith in an overcoming truth, which has made Lieutenant Commander

> *Instead of the theological liberalism and liberation theology he once ingested from the preaching of Jeremiah Wright, the president now sits in the intimacy of Evergreen Chapel and hears the themes familiar to the Baptist pulpit. And it is changing Obama.*

Cash such a force in Obama's life. It has come largely through the chaplain's sermons. "You don't have a heart beating in your chest if you don't feel [it] when you hear this man talk," Brigadier General Frederick Padilla, once Cash's commander, has said. And President Obama seems to agree. Cash "delivers as powerful a sermon as I've heard. I really think he's excellent."[13]

This respect for Cash symbolizes the religious shift Obama has experienced. Instead of the theological liberalism and liberation theology he once ingested from the preaching of Jeremiah Wright, the president now sits in the intimacy of Evergreen Chapel and hears the themes familiar to the Baptist pulpit—salvation for the repentant, the inspiration of Scripture, the blessings of God for his servants, the strength and wisdom of heaven for battles to come. And it is changing Obama. As Joel Hunter reports,

The president loves this chaplain, his pastor. It is a pleasant surprise. Because his family is not made to feel on display, they can focus on worship. And they love the sermons. That's the deal. There is something new happening in their lives.[14]

Thus, while his critics may not accept it, his supporters may be surprised by it, and the majority of Americans may not understand it, Barack Obama is undergoing a religious transformation while in office—one that has been achieved through the ministry of his new band of brothers and his fiercely devoted pastor at Camp David. The more this story becomes known, of course, the more it will likely become fuel for political contention—much like all other matters in Obama's life. Yet, viewed apart from the fray, it is a tender tale—of a young black man in his twenties searching for a spiritual father, of a gifted young ruler longing for a nobler spirituality than he had known, of a president deepened religiously by a band of men who defy politics and hardship to serve the will of God.

THIS, THEN, IS THE SEA CHANGE IN OBAMA'S PERSONAL religious life. What confuses and frustrates his critics, though, is that there seems to be no similar change in the president's politics. They would hope otherwise. They would hope that if Obama is undergoing a move away from the worldview of Jeremiah Wright and a meager devotional life that it might be reflected in his policies, might be accompanied by a more faith-based, more traditional, perhaps more principled way of governing. Here, they find little of encouragement.

Among these critics is Jerome Corsi, the Harvard PhD. who wrote *Unfit for Command*, creating the "Swiftboat" controversy that helped torpedo John Kerry's presidential run in 2004, and also *The Obama Nation*, which raised questions about Barack Obama's birth, religion, political affiliations, and policies during the 2008 presidential race. Both books were *New York Times* bestsellers. Both helped to set the rhetorical tone of the political Right. Both have continued to shape popular perceptions of their subjects.

Of Obama's faith, both the faith with which he entered office and that which has resulted from his religious deepening since, Corsi is deeply suspicious. Corsi, a Roman Catholic, has said:

> Barack Obama's Christianity is a religion of political convenience. You find in him no orthodox Christian doctrine, a heavy dose of Marxism, a heavy dose of race, but a very poor brand of Christianity. His faith is essentially Marxism transplanted onto a watered-down version of Christianity. I just don't see much fruit that indicates he is a Christian regardless of what he has learned to say or read to the public.[15]

What confirms this for Corsi is Obama's conduct in office.

> He makes a great deal of Ramadan but you have a hard time getting him to put up a crèche in the White House. He doesn't attend national prayer services, hasn't chosen a church in DC, and can't seem to quote the Declaration of Independence

without omitting the name of God. Then, in his first term, religion has been a very minor issue. He doesn't offer any faith-based initiatives that I can see. He does not emphasize prayer days or work comments about God into his speeches. Nevertheless, he does seem to find time to push the abortion agenda about as far as it can be pushed—and the gay agenda and socialist economic agenda. This just isn't what a true man of faith would do.[16]

Corsi suspects that Obama's true spiritual home is somewhere far removed from the Christianity the president claims for himself.

"Obama is rooted in Islam. That's what he was taught as a child and that's what he is most comfortable with. He's the warmest and the fuzziest when he is around Muslims." This, Corsi believes, is shaping perceptions worldwide and even effecting American foreign policy.

> "Obama is rooted in Islam. That's what he was taught as a child and that's what he is most comfortable with. He's the warmest and the fuzziest when he is around Muslims."

In the Middle East, it is widely believed that Obama is a Muslim. They know he has never renounced Islam. And they listen carefully when he appeals to the Muslim world as though it is his native land. In country after country in the Middle

East—in Israel for example—they strongly believe that he does what he has to as a Christian to cover his Islamic faith.[17]

Equally suspicious of Obama, but for different reasons than Corsi, is David Barton, a historian whom *Time* magazine has called "a hero to millions" for his renditions of America's Christian heritage and divine purpose. Barton allows that Obama may be, in some form, Christian but insists that given the administration's policies it doesn't seem to matter.

He might have a Christian faith but it clearly isn't a biblical faith. What difference does it make, politically speaking, if the man is a Christian personally if he doesn't let that Christian faith shape his policies? And Obama clearly does not have biblical policies in any form.

You have to remember, that Obama was schooled in the United Church of Christ denomination for twenty years. He is a perfect reflection of that denomination. It is a classic, liberal, shrinking denomination. They were the first supposedly Christian denomination to ordain gays. They called for abortion on demand two years before abortion was even legal. They even supported partial birth abortion. They endorse the Palestinians above the Jews. They have problems with the "sexist" God of the Bible and so they use "gender neutral" language in their services. They believe in a living Bible and a living Constitution. For them, there are no fixed absolutes, particularly on moral issues.

This background explains much of the Obama presidency, Barton insists:

Obama has offered no change in faith or morals in the White House. The Defense of Marriage Act (DOMA) is an example. He began setting DOMA aside long before he refused to defend it. He did not make it a basis for cabinet level appointments. He did not pursue the means at his disposal to support traditional marriage. Then he abandoned DOMA altogether. He was only being consistent though. In his first six months, he instituted forty-one pro-abortion policies, more so than any other president. This really tells us who this man is.[19]

What also convinces Barton is Obama's clumsiness with statements of faith.

He has misquoted the Declaration of Independence on seven different occasions, leaving the name of God out each time. He has done the same with the national motto. He has said it is *E Pluribus Unum*. It isn't. It is "In God We Trust." He surely knows this, but he refuses to quote it correctly. He has even de-emphasized themes of faith in his own administrative departments. The Office of Faith-Based Initiatives is now a low-level office. In fact, they took that office off of the administration's website the day they came to power. That was a clear signal of their intentions.[20]

What encourages Barton is that political battles to come may provide opportunity to expose what most media outlets refuse to cover—Obama's antireligious bent. "The truth of this is already out there. It has gone viral. There are video clips, blogs, the websites of pro-family groups and conservative news organizations making it known." Will Obama's run for a second term serve this purpose?

> How big an issue Obama's religion becomes will be decided by the opposing candidate. Will the Republican standard bearer have the courage to take the issue on? I'm hopeful, but at this point I don't see a candidate willing to raise this issue to the level it deserves.[21]

THESE, THEN, ARE THE FAULT LINES DEFINED BY OBAMA'S faith. They will not be papered over by time and the distraction of events. They will only grow more stark, more defined, as political conflicts intensify.

The challenge for Obama, if indeed there is a new spiritual dynamic working in his life, will be to bridge between his newfound faith and his politics. This will be demanded by an inquisitive electorate and by his Republican opponents. He must cease being the fragmented man, the exotic figure whose faith, personality, and politics never quite seem to gel. He will have to work toward seamlessness, toward ease of understanding for those who look on. Mystery and celebrity will not do in the days to come. He must appear as a leader fully formed, as a man honed by experience, seasoned by adversity, tempered by reflection.

It is possible that he has, as his critics allege, learned his politics, in part, from radicals, from former terrorists and from the left edge of American politics. Yet the country has been told this and has chosen to trust that he has matured, that he is

> *The challenge for Obama, if indeed there is a new spiritual dynamic working in his life, will be to bridge between his newfound faith and his politics.*

not now as he has been. Americans are nearly always willing to overlook and move on. Still, if the president is indeed a new man of faith, he will have to bring this to the fore and show the country how his beliefs undergird his brand of leadership. There will be new faith forums. There will be new crises that require religious explanation. These will force questions. What is the connection between Obama's love of Scripture and his view of abortion, for example? How does he make a biblical case for refusing to support the biblical view of marriage? How does he understand same-sex marriage from a foundation of faith?

The secular will not care. His unswerving loyalists will not insist upon answers. His opponents, though, and those swing voters he will need in order to win a second term, will need to understand. Then we shall see if a new Barack Obama indeed emerges. Will it be the religiously passionate Barack Obama, the man who ministered to his hurting friend in an hour of crisis? Or will it be the cool, practiced politico who takes the stage. This is the question that will define elections, that will define the direction of the nation, and that will define who Barack Obama will be—even *coram deo*, in the face of God.

6

A Time to Heal

IT IS THE HEALERS WHO ARE BEST REMEMBERED, THOSE who teach us to free the better angels of our nature and to live beyond the limitations of our lesser selves. The healers are great-hearts, lovers, expansive souls who show us the path to the world we've hoped for, who teach us that we can make our high-flying rhetoric into living, earthly reality.

They tend to come after bruising, bloody seasons, and yet they seem immune to the rage and vengeance of lesser men. They know how to grasp forgiveness and largeness of heart, having usually mined these traits from the dark valleys of their own lives. Thankfully, they rise to grace a larger stage and then heal their land and their people with the truths hard won in less visible days. Nations, then, are unified. Political strife is transformed into statesmanship. Races are ennobled and readied to belong to a larger whole. Men and women are freed from the grip of the petty and the small. This is what healers do.

Abraham Lincoln comes to mind. From the depths of a life haunted by the deepest emotional depression, he wrung a generosity of soul that resisted the fierce hatreds of his time. He appointed his political rivals as members of his cabinet, pleaded for forgiveness as the Civil War drew to an end, and called his nation to greatness in grand sentences that live on:

> With malice toward none; with charity for all; with firmness in the right, as God gives us to see the right, let us strive on to finish the work we are in; to bind up the nation's wounds; to care for him who shall have borne the battle, and for his widow, and his orphan—to do all which may achieve and cherish a just and lasting peace, among ourselves, and with all nations.[1]

Abraham Lincoln was a healer. Nelson Mandela was too. Though imprisoned for terrorism against a racist state, Mandela emerged decades later to lead in the healing of his land. "If there are dreams about a beautiful South Africa," he once said, "there are also roads that lead to their goal. Two of these roads could be named Goodness and Forgiveness."

There is, of course, Martin Luther King Jr., who might have stood on the steps of the Lincoln Memorial in 1963 and vented the rage of his people. Instead, he urged a faith that would "transform the jangling discords of our nation into a beautiful symphony of brotherhood." He was a healer.

And some healers heal by deed if not by word. Only at the funeral of former President Gerald Ford did we come to understand what we should have known long before: that Ford was a man of exceptional goodness who "drew out the poisons released by Vietnam and Watergate."[2] He did not live in an age as epic as Lincoln's nor did he possess King's rhetorical gifts, but he was a healer by character and condition of soul and at a time when his nation needed him but did not understand the sign of grace that he was.

There are others, of course: the Gandhis and the Washingtons, men like Desmond Tutu and William Wilberforce, women like Benazir Bhutto and Golda Meir. They will all be well remembered, for warriors are remembered with awe and statesmen with respect, but it is the healers who are remembered with love.

~

IT WAS WILLIAM SHAKESPEARE WHO WROTE IN *JULIUS Caesar* that

> There is a tide in the affairs of men,
> Which taken at the flood, leads on to fortune;
> Omitted, all the voyage of their life
> Is bound in shallows and in miseries.
> On such a full sea are we now afloat;
> And we must take the current when it serves,
> Or lose our ventures.

He was saying that fate sometimes offers opportunity that must be recognized and then embraced. To do so leads to glory. To fail to recognize the destined moment is to remain in the shallows, in the immobility of low tide, in the miserable contemplation of what might have been.

> *The presence of Barack Obama on the national stage, politics aside, provides an opportunity for the contemplation of national ills and conflicts that may, if we are wise, lead us to fulfill the potential of a destined moment.*

The presence of Barack Obama on the national stage, politics aside, provides an opportunity for the contemplation of national ills and conflicts that may, if we are wise, lead us to fulfill the potential of a destined moment—and this at a time of great turmoil in our history. This opportunity is not one that Obama consciously offers, but rather one that his presence announces, not one that he intends; but rather one that he symbolizes even for his political opponents.

Yet this opportunity is not likely to be answered by politics and by the doings of government. Far from it. We should remember the words of columnist George Will, who wrote, "There is hardly a page of American history that does not refute that insistence, so characteristic of the political class, on the primacy of politics in the making of history."[3] Therefore, Will contends, "Almost nothing is as important as almost every-thing in Washington is made to appear. And the importance of a Washington event is apt to be inversely proportional to the attention it receives."[4] And this is as the founding generation expected it to be, for as Patrick Henry stated, "Liberty necessi-tates the diminutization of political ambition and concern. Liberty necessitates concentration on other matters than mere civil governance."[5] No, government is not likely to answer the opportunity now offered to our generation. Oddly, though, it is politics that is pushing onto the national stage the issues that, rightly treated, may lead to a new day in our history.

Consider for example, the matter of race. As long as Barack Obama and his presidency live in history, so too shall the name of Reverend Jeremiah A. Wright. It cannot be otherwise. Perhaps for generations Americans will ask how Obama could have lis-tened to such a man for twenty years and what impact the enraged reverend had upon the Obama administration, despite his imposed distance. Yet even here is an opportunity wrapped in disguising turmoil. Could it be that what the Wright affair offers the nation is an opportunity, a strategic moment for heal-ing and grace? Could it be that, beyond the politics of the moment, there is Shakespeare's tide to be taken at the flood, an open door of healing for the land?

UNDERSTANDABLY, ONCE AMERICANS HEARD SNIPPETS OF Wright's sermons and caught his manner before the press, they concluded he was a madman, a nut, a racist older black man hopefully passing with all those like him from the scene. Politics demanded that Obama distance himself from the man—his pastor, his mentor, his friend—and so he did, claiming, as some termed it, "the crazy old uncle defense": that Wright had once been brilliant and gifted but now was descending into the foolishness all can see. It was painful to watch and most Americans will hold it in memory as a troubling oddity in yet another cycle of crazy in American politics.

Yet Jeremiah Wright is not insane. He is an educated man with four earned degrees, respected in his church and his denomination, who has been an honored voice of black America. When the Clinton administration sought to cleanse both itself and the nation of the Lewinsky scandal, Wright was among those invited to the White House. When black churches nationwide yearn to experience spiritual revival, they often call Jeremiah Wright. When leading seminaries wish to understand black religious thought, they call, among others, Jeremiah Wright. Despite his often unusual behavior before the national press—surely the antics of a hurt and angry man—all the evidence indicates that this is a man in his right mind articulating a message shared by millions. To claim him crazy and dismiss him from the scene without a hearing is to miss an opportunity to heal a grievous, festering wound.

What Wright contends is that the United States government is more often a force of oppression than of good. He argues that there are national sins that must be addressed, wrongs inflicted by our government on the helpless at home and abroad that displease God and—if the biblical law of sowing and reaping is true—may bring ill on Americans at home; their "chickens coming home to roost." So rigorous is he in exposing these wrongs, so committed is he to resisting the oppressor in aid of the oppressed, that he told Obama—his friend, his parishioner—in 2007, "If you get elected, November the 5th I'm coming after you, because you'll be representing a government whose policies grind under people."[6]

And what are these national wrongs? There is slavery, of course, and the ill treatment of Native Americans. There is also the charge of police oppression in America's inner cities. These are not unexpected. Yet Wright goes further. He charges that his government commits acts of medical abuse on blacks. He believes that people of color are sacrificed in immoral wars abroad and that those very wars spread misery and murder throughout the world. He argues that even our most revered presidents lied to their fellow citizens and that time and again wickedness more than righteousness infuses American foreign policy. And he is not alone. These sentiments sound from black pulpits throughout the country, as well as from the scholars and writers who share their cause.

We should pause to reflect that if half of these charges are true, they ought to be the concern of more than just black ministers. Any citizen who takes American values to heart should be both astonished and ashamed. Any faith that values compassion and holds human life as made in a divine image should be appalled and seek to make amends. Perhaps, if even half of Wright's charges are true, his claims present an opportunity to heal historic wounds. Perhaps this is a call to be more Christian than Republican, more American than Democrat, more noble and righteous than crassly and callously political. Perhaps, too, this is an opportunity to hear truth from the mouths of our critics, to allow them to be the unpaid guardians of our national soul.

> *Wright's suspicions that his government may not have his race's best interest at heart are not fantasy and the compassionate in American society should try to understand why.*

For the fact is that some of what Wright says is true and more than the matters of slavery and native peoples and police behavior, all of which are well known. The fact is that the American government has engaged in medical abuse of blacks. Wright's suspicions that his government may not have his race's best interest at heart are not fantasy and the compassionate in American society should try to understand why.

From 1932 until 1972, more than four hundred black men with syphilis from Macon County, Alabama, were enrolled in a medical study in which treatment for their affliction was denied. Called the Tuskegee Syphilis Study, the program was operated by the U.S. Public Health Service. In the study, men with syphilis were not told of their true disease, but were informed that they were being treated for *bad blood*, a local term used to describe a variety of illnesses like anemia and fatigue. Even after 1947, when penicillin became the standard cure for syphilis, the antibiotic was withheld so that researchers could study how syphilis spreads and kills. As a result, dozens of men died, wives and children were infected, and the study continued until 1972 when public health workers leaked the story to the press. The next year, in 1973, a class-action lawsuit led to a $9 million settlement that was shared by the remaining participants.

The lesson was not lost on Jeremiah Wright's generation, though other abuses had already driven the message home: our government will allow black men to die as guinea pigs for medical research. This message embedded in the hearts of black Americans just as Wright took the lead of Trinity United Church of Christ, just as black theology was beginning to shape the African American church.

Twenty-four years after the experiment ended, President Bill Clinton apologized for what his government had done. Saying that the Tuskegee Syphilis Study was "deeply, profoundly, morally wrong," Clinton concluded:

> To the survivors, to the wives and family members, the children and the grandchildren, I say what you know: No power on Earth can give you back the lives lost, the pain suffered, the years of internal torment and anguish. What was done cannot be undone. But we can end the silence. We can stop turning our heads away. We can look at you in the eye and finally say,

on behalf of the American people: what the United States government did was shameful. And I am sorry.[7]

The meaning here is not that everything Wright contends is
true, but that there is enough truth for a compassionate people,
for a people who care about the culture of their nation more
than political advantage, to examine and treat redemptively.
Surely, it is appropriate for the lies of government to be
addressed, for example, much as Clinton addressed the immorality of the Tuskegee Study. Wright has suggested also that
Franklin Roosevelt knew in advance about the Japanese attack
on Pearl Harbor but lied to the American people. Commentators
across the political spectrum, from FOX to CNN, guffawed in
derision. Yet this view has long been discussed among serious
academics, at least since Charles A. Beard wrote his *President
Roosevelt and the Coming of the War, 1941* in 1948. It is not a view
widely shared by modern historians, but it is academically
credible enough to make us hesitate in dismissing Wright as a
fool. Instead, his views ought to be heard, understood as those
of a people within America, and addressed in an effort to heal.

Still, what offends many Americans is that Wright has
sounded his complaints from a Christian pulpit. Here there is a
misunderstanding of the black church experience. From the days
of slavery until now, the black church in America has seldom
been just a Sunday morning meeting. It has been, in the earliest
days, the few hours on a Sunday morning that slaves could call
their own; to worship, yes, but also to hear the latest news, to

plan for the good of the community, and to insulate as a people against the times. Later, when laws allowed, the black church became a prophetic voice against injustice, taking as its mission both to save individuals and to confront society with the will of the living God. This prophetic tradition, this addressing of both the spiritual and the societal, was what moved the black church to the forefront of the battle for civil rights and gave rise to men like Martin Luther King Jr. Consider, for example, King's understanding of the role between the church and the state.

> The church must be reminded that it is not the master or the servant of the state, but rather the conscience of the state. It must be the guide and the critic of the state, and never its tool. If the church does not recapture its prophetic zeal, it will become an irrelevant social club without moral or spiritual authority. If the church does not participate actively in the struggle for peace and for economic and racial justice, it will forfeit the loyalty of millions and cause men everywhere to say that it has atrophied its will. But if the church will free itself from the shackles of a deadening status quo, and, recovering its great historic mission, will speak and act fearlessly and insistently in terms of justice and peace, it will enkindle the imagination of mankind and fire the souls of men, imbuing them with a glowing and ardent love for truth, justice, and peace.[8]

This is indicative of the tradition out of which Jeremiah Wright speaks, and a society as great as America believes herself to be ought to be able to hear him. When he suggests that poverty is at the same rate as when Martin Luther King Jr. launched his Poor People's Campaign in 1968, it is a point a great people ought to consider. When he argues that the sufferings of Native Americans should be addressed with more than the proceeds from gambling casinos, a righteous people ought to hear. And when his parishioner, Barack Obama, claims that

> the path to a more perfect union means acknowledging that what ails the African American community does not just exist in the minds of black people; that the legacy of discrimination—and current incidents of discrimination, while less overt than in the past—are real and must be addressed,

a people intending to be a great society must try to understand and act.[9]

Yet this is how the story—and the hoped-for healing it portends—continues: with a new generation. In his "A More Perfect Union" speech, in which he explained his history with Jeremiah Wright, Obama described himself in generational terms. Wright was of an age of blacks, he said, for whom

> *Wright was of an age of blacks, he said, for whom "the memories of humiliation and doubt and fear have not gone away, nor has the anger and the bitterness of those years."*

"the memories of humiliation and doubt and fear have not gone away, nor has the anger and the bitterness of those years." Obama proclaimed himself a member of a new generation, a younger people committed to "embracing the burdens of our past without becoming the victims of our past." A change had come, he offered, and a new generation of African Americans was now taking the reins.

It may well be that this same new generation's approach to faith will also provide an opportunity for American society. For decades the faith-based approach to American politics has been divided into two nearly armed camps. The first is the Religious Left—rooted in theological liberalism, enthusiastic about employing the mechanisms of government to achieve righteous ends, careful to keep moral judgments about homosexuality or abortion from the hopefully neutral public square. Then there is the Religious Right—rooted in an "original intent" approach to Scripture, suspicious of government as a means of social good, determined to man the barricades of biblical morality in the land.

The former has been championed by Barack Obama. The latter by George W. Bush. The former has been fathered by Ceasar Chávez and Martin Luther King Jr. The latter by Jerry Falwell and Ronald Reagan. The former would make compassion the measure of all government acts. The latter would make individual freedom the most sacred right. The former reads the

Bible to affirm the social justice of the Old Testament prophets and to proclaim, "let justice roll on like a river, righteousness like a never-failing stream."[10] The latter would prefer "if a man won't work he shouldn't eat" and "proclaim liberty throughout all the land."[11]

And so it goes.

> In a holy book in which the cause of poverty is mentioned more than two thousand times, is government forbidden from tending the needs of the poor?

A new generation, however, weary of the deadlock and the war of sacred texts, asks the questions that defy the categories of old. In a holy book in which the cause of poverty is mentioned more than two thousand times, is government forbidden from tending the needs of the poor? In a holy book in which the unborn are described as leaping in response to good tidings or being filled with the Holy Spirit in the womb, is any sanction for terminating a pregnancy to be found? Is poverty purely a function of bad character or can it also come from oppression and injustice and greed? Should a people seek only to be rich? Is peace the hope only of the weak, or is peace the will of God for man? Is the most relevant verse "love thy neighbor" or is it "obey the Lord?"

Standing at the crossroads of these questions is Barack Obama. He has championed the Religious Left, and yet he has undergone a change since his earlier, more radical days. He has put down roots more deeply in the Christian tradition, has consumed more fully the meaning of biblical truth. He now has opportunity to articulate his social vision in terms of a faith he has newly embraced. Perhaps he can bridge the divide between Religious Right and Left and do so by extolling the fully orbed social vision of Scripture that both movements fail to fully appreciate.

We can hope this of Barack Obama because of his unique approach to politics and faith. There have been other Democrats who were religiously fluent, of course. Bill Clinton and Jimmy Carter come to mind. Yet both men seemed to truncate their faith, seemed to erect a wall of separation between faith and practice. Obama's religion infuses his public policy, so that his faith is not just limited to the personal realms of his life, it also informs his public leadership as well. He roots his political liberalism in a theological worldview. In the days to come he may well call others to do the same, much to the challenge of what has come before: the secular Left, the truncated faith of traditional politics, certainly, the now fading Religious Right.

What is certain is that the faith of Barack Obama will not only animate his life and leadership but will continue to give the nation opportunity to confront matters of race and public policy within a framework of religious values. This may offer us, in the midst of our trials, a season of reflection—upon what we have been, upon what God and his will means to us as a people,

opposition, which makes me better than I am alone. What she does for my writing she also does for my life, transforming both by her passion, her joy, and her strength.

The firm she leads, Chartwell Literary Group (www. chartwellliterary.com), is a team of literary experts I cannot live without. It is their sense of a book's spirit, of the creative possibilities of the printed word, that inspires me and helps me see the wonder of books as though for the first time. Under Beverly's wise guidance, Chartwell is becoming a writer's band of brothers and the answer to a publisher's prayer.

Joining her on my immediate team has been Dr. George Grant—older brother, mentor, and friend—who allowed me in this book to critique the very Religious Right he has loved, pastored, chastised, and intellectually led. His graciousness in the face of my views and his patience in the face of my demands on his time are evidence of a character I can only hope to emulate.

Melinda Gales of the Gales Network (www.galesnetwork .com) scheduled the interviews that made this book what it is, while her husband, David, helped me understand the manuscript through his kind but unsparing eyes. Michaela Jackson, research genius and editor, never ceased to remind me that her generation—the young who "do faith like jazz"—cannot be ignored in the Obama story, and I trust that I have captured both the passion and the importance of that tribe in this book. Dimples Kellogg so skillfully edited the manuscript that she left me wondering if I have ever written anything in the true English language. Dan Williamson, David Holland, and Stephen Prather have given wise counsel, and I am grateful to each of these, but for their friendship most of all.

There have been many generous souls willing to speak with me about the themes that touch Barack Obama's life. Chief among these has been Joshua DuBois, head of the Office of Faith-Based and Neighborhood Partnerships. His personal faith, intelligence, love for President Obama, and devotion to faith-based social change has moved me. Dr. Joel Hunter, one of the president's spiritual advisors and pastor of Central Florida's Northland Church, was not only unselfish with his time but tenderly transparent in recounting the story of his granddaughter, Ava, which appears in these pages. I am grateful and trust that grief will not overwhelm.

Jim Wallis of Sojourners helped me understand the cause of social justice and Obama's commitment to it in a lengthy interview that I will always recall with gratitude. Dr. Dwight N. Hopkins of the University of Chicago Divinity School graciously read my treatment of black theology and Jeremiah Wright, taking time to gently help this white man understand. Ambassador Alan Keyes offered his characteristic fire in recounting the Illinois Senate race of 2004, and George Barna showed us why he is one of the true wise men of our age. Professor Paul Kengor of Grove City College offered us insight beyond his seminal *God and Hillary Clinton: A Spiritual Life*, and Guy Rodgers, once national director of Americans of Faith for McCain, helped us understand the man he has served so well. Dr. Jeff Clark, of both Middle Tennessee State University and McLean/Clark in

Washington DC, gave us keen understanding of who Obama is, and Dave Zinati provided unique insight into the reality of the Religious Right. David Barton of Wallbuilders was gracious in explaining his view of Barack Obama and in providing seminal material for this book. I understood, once again, why *Time* magazine has called him a "hero to millions." Dr. Jerome Corsi kindly visited with me just as he was launching another raucous book tour and I appreciate his candor, his scholarship, and his love of good cigars.

I must also thank Trinity United Church of Christ for hosting me so graciously over an Easter weekend, Archbishop Desmond Tutu for his encouraging words, and Malcolm DuPlessis for bringing the archbishop into my life.

Joel Miller has long made working with Thomas Nelson a joy and did so once again during this project. Strategic support of an essential kind has been provided by Jim Laffoon, Brett Fuller, Sam Webb, and Norman Nakanishi. They are friends and fathers, all, and I could not do without them. I wish also to thank Christopher and Tamara Clarke, whose stately home just outside of Washington, DC has proven a welcome haven for this writer.

Finally, deepest appreciation to my children Jonathan and Elizabeth. Though both were busy college students during the writing of this book—Elizabeth a history major at Belmont University, Jonathan a business major at The University of Tennessee—they stir me with their questions, inspire me with their kindness, and touch me with their humor and their joy. A father could ask for no finer children.

Notes

Introduction

1. The Pew Forum on Religion and Public Life, "Growing Number of Americans Say Obama Is a Muslim," August 18, 2010 http://pewforum .org/Politics-and-Elections/Growing-Number-of-Americans-Say-Obama-is-a-Muslim.aspx

2. Author Interview with unnamed White House source, March 16, 2011.

3. Saul Relative, "Huckabee Gaffe Points to that Obama Kenya Muslim Stuff— Again," *Yahoo News*, Thursday, March 3, 2011.

4. Todd Purdum, "Raising Obama," *Vanity Fair*, March 2008.

5. The Barna Group, "Born Again Voters No Longer Favor Republican Candidates," February 4, 2008, 1, http://www.barna.org/FlexPage.aspx?Page=B arnaUpdateNarrow&BarnaUpdateID=291.

6. Adam Nagourney and Megan Thee, "Young Americans Are Leaning Left, New Poll Finds," *New York Times*, June 27, 2007.

Chapter 1—To Walk Between Worlds

1. Janny Scott, "The Long Run: In 2000, a Streetwise Veteran Schooled a Bold Young Obama," *New York Times*, September 9, 2007.

2. Barack Obama, *Dreams from My Father* (New York: Three Rivers Press, 1995), 15.

3. Tim Jones, "Special Report: Making of a Candidate," *Chicago Tribune*, March 27, 2007.

4. Ibid.

5. Obama, *Dreams*, 17.

6. Jones, "Special Report."

7. Paul Johnson, *Modern Times* (New York: HarperCollins, 1983), 479.

8. Ibid.

9. Obama, *Dreams*, 50.

10. Barack Obama, *The Audacity of Hope* (New York: Three Rivers Press, 2006), 204.

11. Abul Ala Maududi, *The Punishment of the Apostate According to Islamic Law* (Lahore: Islamic Publications, 1994), 30–31.

12. Obama, *Dreams*, 58.

13. Ibid., 86.

14. Purdum, "Raising Obama."

15. Sharon Cohen, "Barack Obama Straddles Different Worlds," *USA Today*, December 14, 2007.

16. Obama, *Dreams*, xv.

17. Ibid., 155.

18. Obama, *Audacity*, 206.

19. Obama, *Dreams*, 287.

20. Obama, *Audacity*, 209.

21. Ibid., 208.

Chapter 2—My House, Too

1. Tim Grieve, "Left Turn at Saddleback Church," Salon.com, December 2, 2006.

2. Iva E. Carruthers, Frederick D. Haynes II, and Jeremiah A. Wright Jr., eds., *Blow the Trumpet in Zion* (Minneapolis: Fortress Press, 2005), 5.

3. Ibid.

4. Ibid.

5. Ibid., 6.

6. Ibid., 5.

7. Manya A. Brachear, "Rev. Jeremiah A. Wright, Jr.: Pastor Inspires Obama's 'Audacity,'" *Chicago Tribune*, January 21, 2007.

8. Luke 4:18 NIV.

9. James H. Cone, *A Black Theology of Liberation: Twentieth Anniversary Edition* (New York: Orbis, 1986), 45–46.

10. James H. Cone, *God of the Oppressed* (New York: Orbis, 1997), xi.

11. Cone, *A Black Theology of Liberation*, 38.

12. Ibid., 35.

13. Ibid., 28.

14. Ibid., 25.

15. William A. Von Hoene Jr., "Rev. Wright in a Different Light," *Chicago Tribune*, March 26, 2008.

Chapter 3—Faith Fit for the Age

1. Obama, *Audacity*, 208.

2. Cathleen Falsani, "I Have a Deep Faith," *Chicago Sun Times*, April 5, 2005; Sarah Pulliam and Ted Olson, "Q&A: Barack Obama," *Christianity Today*, January 2008, Web-only edition, http://www .christianitytoday.com/ct/2008/januaryweb-only/104-32.0.html.

3. Obama, *Audacity*, 208.

4. Barack Obama, "Call to Renewal" keynote address, Wednesday, June 28, 2006, Washington DC.

5. Obama, *Audacity*, 206.

6. Ibid., 208.

7. Ibid.

8. Ibid.

9. John K. Wilson, *Barack Obama: This Improbable Quest* (Boulder: Paradigm Publishers, 2008), 136.

10. Ibid., 137.

11. Ibid., 138.

12. Ibid.

13. Obama, "Call to Renewal."

14. Falsani, "I Have a Deep Faith."

15. Obama, *Audacity*, 204.

16. Falsani, "I Have a Deep Faith."

17. Wilson, *Barack Obama*, 138.

18. Obama, *Audacity*, 226.

19. Wilson, *Barack Obama*, 139.

20. Ibid.

21. Falsani, "I Have a Deep Faith."

22. Obama, *Audacity*, 222.

23. 2 Tim. 3:16 KJV.

24. Obama, *Audacity*, 224.

25. Barack Obama, "On My Faith and My Church," March 14, 2008, http://www.realclearpolitics.com/articles/2008/03/on_my_faith_and_my_church.html.

Chapter 4—The Altars of State

1. The details of this vignette are based on the description of Abraham Lincoln's congressional race against Rev. Peter Cartwright in Carl Sandburg's *Abraham Lincoln: The Prairie Years and the War Years* (New York: Harcourt, Brace & World, Inc., 1954), 83–84.

2. Obama, *Audacity*, 46–47.

3. Ibid., 18.

4. David Mendell, *Obama: From Promise to Power* (New York: Amistad, 2007), 261.

5. "Alan Keyes," Race 4 2008, http://race42008.com/alan-keyes.

6. Obama, *Audacity*, 209.

7. Ibid., 210.

8. John Chase and Liam Ford, "Senate Debate Gets Personal," *Chicago Tribune*, October 22, 2004.

9. Liam Ford and David Mendell, "Jesus Wouldn't Vote for Obama, Keyes Says," *Chicago Tribune*, September 8, 2004.

10. Ibid.

11. Ibid.

12. Ibid.

13. Obama, *Audacity*, 211.

14. Obama, "Call to Renewal."

15. Ibid.

16. The speech served as the rough draft for the chapter on faith in Obama's *The Audacity of Hope*, published the same year.

17. E. J. Dionne, Op-Ed., *Washington Post*, June 30, 2006.

18. Peter Wood, "Obama's Prayer: Wooing Evangelicals," *National Review*, July 6, 2006, http://article.nationalreview.com?q=ZTMzNDU5ZDU4ZjhiYTkxMzhhNTk3Y2M5MmRhMmJkY2U=.

19. A compilation from Hegel by Karl R. Popper, *The Open Society and Its Enemies*, 4th ed., 2 vols. (Princeton: Princeton University Press, 1963), 2:31.

20. Falsani, "I Have a Deep Faith."

21. Will Herberg, *Catholic-Protestant-Jew*, rev. ed. (Garden City, NY: Doubleday Anchor, 1960), 260.

22. Herbert Schlossberg, *Idols for Destruction* (Nashville: Thomas Nelson, 1983), 252.

23. Ibid., 251.

24. Pulliam and Olsen, "Q&A: Barack Obama."

25. Amanda B. Carpenter, "Obama More Pro-Choice Than NARAL," *Human Events*, December 25, 2006, http://www.humanevents.com/article.php?id=18647.

26. NARAL release, 6/13, as quoted in "NARAL Says It Does Not Oppose Born Alive Infants Act, Calls Bill 'Trap' to Put Abortion-Rights Supporters on Defensive" in Kaiser Daily Women's Health Policy section, Daily Reports, June 20, 2001, http://www.kaisernetwork.org/daily_reports/rep_index.cfm?DR_ID=5334.

27. Carpenter, "Obama More Pro-Choice Than NARAL."

28. Ibid.

29. Obama, *Audacity*, 223–24.

Chapter 5—A New Band of Brothers

1. Larry Rohter and Michael Luo, "Groups Respond to Obama's Call for National Discussion about Race," *New York Times*, March 20, 2008, http://www.nytimes.com/2008/03/20/us/politics/20race.html.

2. Author interview with Joel Hunter, April 27, 2011.

3. Ibid.

4. Alex Altman, "Joshua DuBois: Obama's Pastor-in-Chief," *Time*, February 6, 2009.

5. Author interview with Joshua DuBois, February 28, 2011.

6. Ibid.

7. Hunter interview.

8. Ibid.

9. Ibid.

10. DuBois Interview.

11. Jacqueline L. Salmon, "The Pastor Who Has Obama's Attention," *The Washington Post*, October 14, 2009.

12. Ibid.

13. Ibid.

14. Hunter Interview.

15. Author Interview with Jerome Corsi, March 22, 2011.

16. Ibid.

17. Ibid.

18. Author Interview with David Barton, March 22, 2011.

19. Ibid.

20. Ibid.

21. Ibid.

Chapter 6—A Time to Heal

1. Abraham Lincoln, Second Inaugural Address, March 4, 1865.

2. Richard Norton Smith, *Eulogy for President Ford*, January 3, 2007.

3. *Nashville Banner*, January 25, 1993.

4. *Washington Post*, July 5, 1990.

5. Michael Drummond, *Participatory Democracy: A New Federalism in the Making* (New York: L.T. Carnell and Sons, 1923), 22.

6. Jeremiah A. Wright Jr., National Press Club speech, April 28, 2008.

7. "Remembering the Tuskegee Experiment," NPR, http://www.npr.org/ programs/morning/features/2002/jul/Tuskegee/.

8. Martin Luther King Jr., "A Knock at Midnight," in *A Knock at Midnight: Inspiration from the Great Sermons of Reverend Martin Luther King, Jr.* (New York: Grand Central Publishing, 2000), 72–73.

9. Barack Obama, "A More Perfect Union," speech delivered March 18, 2008.

10. Amos 5:24, NIV.

11. 2 Thessalonians 3:10, Leviticus 25:10 NKJV.

Bibliography

Anyabwile, Thabiti M. *The Decline of African American Theology: From Biblical Faith to Cultural Captivity.* Downers Grove, IL: Academic, 2007.

Barna, George, and Harry R. Jackson Jr. *High Impact African-American Churches.* Ventura, CA: Regal, 2008.

Carruthers, Iva E., Frederick D. Haynes III, and Jeremiah A. Wright Jr., eds. *Blow the Trumpet in Zion: Global Vision and Action for the 21st-Century Black Church.* Minneapolis: Fortress Press, 2005.

Cone, James H. *Risks of Faith: The Emergence of a Black Theology of Liberation, 1968–1998.* Boston: Beacon Press, 1999.

Corsi, Jerome. *The Obama Nation: Leftist Politics and the Cult of Personality.* New York: Simon and Schuster, 2008.

———. *A Black Theology of Liberation: Twentieth Anniversary Edition.* Maryknoll, NY: Orbis Books, 1986.

Dougherty, Steve. *Hopes and Dreams: The Story of Barack Obama.* New York: Black Dog and Leventhal Publishers, 2007.

Kengor, Paul. *God and Hillary Clinton: A Spiritual Life.* New York: HarperCollins, 2007.

McCain, John, and Mark Salter. *Faith of My Fathers: A Family Memoir.* New York: Random House, 1999.

Mansfield, Stephen. *The Faith of George W. Bush.* New York: Penguin, 2003.

Mendell, David. *Obama: From Promise to Power*. New York: Amistad, 2007.

Obama, Barack. *The Audacity of Hope: Thoughts on Reclaiming the American Dream*. New York: Three Rivers Press, 2006.

———. *Dreams from My Father: A Story of Race and Inheritance*. New York: Three Rivers Press, 1995.

Steele, Shelby. *A Bound Man: Why We Are Excited About Obama and Why He Can't Win*. New York: Free Press, 2008.

Wallis, Jim. *The Great Awakening: Reviving Faith & Politics in a Post-Religious Right America*. New York: HarperCollins, 2008.

Wilson, John K. *Barack Obama: This Improbable Quest*. Boulder: Paradigm, 2007.

About the Author

STEPHEN MANSFIELD IS THE *NEW YORK TIMES* BEST-selling author of *The Faith of George W. Bush*, *The Faith of the American Soldier*, *Then Darkness Fled: The Liberating Wisdom of Booker T. Washington*, and *Never Give In: The Extraordinary Character of Winston Churchill*, among other works of history and biography. Founder of both The Mansfield Group, a research and communications firm, and Chartwell Literary Group, which creates and manages literary projects, Stephen is also in wide demand as a lecturer and inspirational speaker. For more information, log on to www.MansfieldGroup.com.

Index

NOTE: Page numbers followed by *f* refer to figures.

devotional delivery system, on Blackberry, 125
Diallo, Amadou, 120
Dionne, E.J., 99
displacement, xx
divorce of parents, ix, 12
Dobson, James, xxii
doubt, 58–59
Dreams from My Father (Obama), x, xii, 26
DuBois, Joshua, 112, 119–125
Dunham, Ann. *See* Soetoro, Ann Dunham
Dunham, Madelyn Payne, 81*f*
  on church hypocrisy, 4–5
  and divinity of Jesus, 9
  work during WW II, 6
Dunham, Stanley, 5, 81*f*
  death, x
  enlistment in army in WW II, 6
  search for frontier, 11
Durbin, Dick, xvii

E

East Shore Unitarian Church (Seattle), 8
Easter speech by Obama, xii
education of Obama
  Columbia University, 24
  English lessons, 21
  Harvard Law School, x
  mother's efforts, 21
  Occidental University, 24
  Punahou School (Hawaii), ix, 22–24
  Roman Catholic influence in, 16
Episcopal Church Bishop, prayer at
  inauguration, xii
eternal punishment, Obama and traditional
  view, 61
evangelical voters, political positions, xxiii
evangelism, vocabulary of, 57
Evergreen Chapel, xiv, 131
execution of *murtadd* (apostate), 19

F

faith, 104
  of Lincoln, political attacks on, 87–89
  sincerity of, xxvii
  use in politics, 99
  ways of finding God, 53
  as work in progress, 63
faith-based politics, xix. *See also* Religious Left;
  Religious Right
  and Keyes/Obama Senate race, 93–94
  Progressive movement, 3

faith community, Obama decision to join,
  29–30
faith of Obama, xviii–xix
  challenge of connecting with politics,
    140–141
  conversion experience, 53–59, 62–63
  crisis, 26
  critics, 135–140
  diversity in childhood, 16, 18
  doubt, 58–59
  individuals influencing, 118. *See also*
    spiritual advisors to Obama
  intellectual approach, 28
  Islam encouraged by Lolo, 16–17
  in Jesus, 54, 62, 130
  Muslim question in childhood, 18–20
  and political views, 67
  prayer life, 61, 85*f*
  prayer with Hunter, 115–117
  religious world view of early life, 4
  survey on American views of, xi
  transformation during presidency, xxvi
  unorthodox spirituality, xxiv
"fall out," 56
Falwell, Jerry, xxii, 155
family, spiritual for Obama, 68–70
fatwa (religious decree), risk for Obama, 20
"First Amendment sanity," 98
Five Fundamental Principles (Indonesia), 14
folk Islam, 4, 17
Ford, Gerald, 145
forgiveness, 144
Foubert, Val, 7
friendship of Obama, 111–117
"From Poverty to Opportunity" conference
  speech, 95–99

G

gay and lesbian singles, Trinity outreach to, 36
Gingrich, Newt, 75
Giuliani, Rudy, xxii
goals, need for, 24
God
  guiding Obama's relationship with,
    118–119
  Obama's belief on path to, 60
  state as, 103
  ways of finding, 53
  Wilson on Obama's view, 61
government, religious conservatives resistence
  to bloated, 102

HILLSBORO PUBLIC LIBRARIES
Hillsboro, OR
Member of Washington County
COOPERATIVE LIBRARY SERVICES